Test Your Grammar and Usage

Cambridge First Certificate

Peter Watcyn-Jones

PENGUIN BOOKS

To Nina and Thomas O'Furey

PENGUIN BOOKS

Published by the Penguin Group
Penguin Books Ltd, 27 Wrights Lane, London W8 5TZ, England
Penguin Books USA Inc,. 375 Hudson Street, New York 10014, USA
Penguin Books Australia Ltd, Ringwood, Victoria, Australia
Penguin Books Canada Ltd, 10 Alcorn Avenue, Toronto, Ontario, Canada M4V 3B2
Penguin Books (NZ) Ltd, 182–90 Wairau Road, Auckland 10, New Zealand

Penguin Books Ltd, Registered Offices: Harmondsworth, Middlesex, England

Published by Penguin Books 1996
10 9 8 7 6 5 4 3 2

Text copyright © Peter Watcyn-Jones 1996
Illustrations copyright © Gordon Thompson 1996
All rights reserved

The moral right of the author and illustrator has been asserted

Printed in England by Clays Ltd, St Ives plc
Set in 9.25/13.5pt Monophoto Times

ACKNOWLEDGEMENTS

The following activities are based on copyright material: 5 and 14 are based on texts from *Urban Myths* by Phil Healey and Rick Glanvill, London, Virgin Books, 1992; 32 is adapted from texts in *World Famous Weird News Stories* by Colin Wilson, Damon Wilson and Rowan Wilson, London, Magpie Books Ltd, 1994; 30 and 43 are based on texts from *Beyond Belief* by Ron Lyon and Jenny Paschall, London, Stanley Paul & Co Ltd, 1993; 34 is from 'Smoking "will kill one million people"' by Angella Johnson, the *Guardian*, 20 September 1994; 42 is from 'Safer driving with hands off' by Alfred Lee, the *Sunday Express*, 27 March 1994; 44 is based on texts from *Urban Myths Unplugged* by Phil Healey and Rick Glanvill, London, Virgin Books, 1994; 45 is adapted from *It Can't be True*, London, Treasure Press, 1983.

CONTENTS

INTRODUCTION

Test Your Grammar and Usage: Cambridge First Certificate is a new book in the Penguin *Test Your...* series and is aimed at students studying for the Cambridge First Certificate examination, though it is equally suitable for any student at intermediate level and above.

There are fifty tests altogether, ranging from tests on specific grammatical points (verb tenses, prepositions, definite and indefinite articles, phrasal verbs, etc.) to tests similar to those found in Paper 3 of the new Cambridge First Certificate examination, where grammar and vocabulary are tested more indirectly (sentence-changing, cloze tests, word-building, etc.) Where possible I have tried to keep the 'look' and 'feel' of the tests used in the examination, including the use throughout of the numbers 0 and 00 to show all examples.

The book can either be used in the classroom or for self-study. To facilitate the latter, a key is included at the back of the book.

In common with the books in the Test Your Vocabulary series, the tests in this book are varied, stimulating and enjoyable and should prove to be a useful complement to any First Certificate course.

1 Sentence-changing 1

Complete the second sentence so that it has a similar meaning to the first sentence, using the word given. **Do not change the word given.** You must use between two and five words, including the word given. There is an example at the beginning (0).

0 This hotel is full.
vacancies
There *are no vacancies at* this hotel.

1 We were surprised to see Pamela at the party.
expect
We .... to see Pamela at the party.

2 Everyone has heard about the canals in Amsterdam.
famous
Amsterdam .... canals.

3 If you pay no attention to him, he'll soon go away.
notice
If you .... him, he'll soon go away.

4 John Lennon was forty when he died.
age
John Lennon .... forty.

5 You can stay with my sister if you're ever in Brighton.
put
My sister will .... if you're ever in Brighton.

6 She didn't say goodbye when she left.
without
She .... goodbye.

7 'I'm sorry I'm late,' he said.
apologized
He .... late.

8 It's possible that they didn't get the message in time.
  might
  They .... the message in time.

9 I haven't smoked for six years.
  gave
  Six years .... smoking.

10 It was wrong of you to steal those apples from Mrs Brown's garden.
   should
   You .... those apples from Mrs Brown's garden.

11 It's a four-hour journey from Swansea to London.
   travel
   It .... from Swansea to London.

12 I don't really want to leave yet.
   rather
   I .... leave yet.

2 The definite and indefinite article

In the following sentences put in *a*, *an* or *the*, but only where necessary.

1 .... Isle of Wight is .... island off .... south coast of .... England.

2 Would you like to see .... picture of .... village I lived in when I was .... child?

3 .... President of .... United States lives in .... White House in .... Washington D.C.

4 .... Nelson's Column is in .... Trafalgar Square, quite near .... National Gallery.

5 Her brother is .... musician. He plays .... flute in .... orchestra. He has been doing this since he left .... school at .... age of eighteen.

6 .... Doctor Williams works in .... large hospital in .... North Wales, not far from .... Town Hall.

7 Shall we go for .... walk in .... Hyde Park this afternoon or shall we go and see .... Van Gogh exhibition at .... Tate Gallery instead?

8 'Do British people shake .... hands when they meet?'
'Yes, sometimes, but not as often as .... Swedes do.'

9 What .... awful weather! I thought you said .... French Riviera was always hot and sunny. .... rain and storms of .... past few days are more typical of .... Britain than .... Mediterranean.

10 My sister lives in .... old house in .... Gloucester Place. She's got .... small flat there on .... top floor.

3 One word only 1

Read the sentences below and think of the word which best fits each space. Use only **one word** in each space. There is an example at the beginning (0).

0 I need ....*some*..... milk. I haven't got ....*any*..... left.

1 It's .... easier to learn to play the guitar .... a teacher .... by trying to teach yourself.

2 She has .... living in Brighton .... 1991.

3 .... he first lived in Italy it took him a long time to get .... to driving .... the right.

4 'How .... do you go jogging?'
   'Oh, about once .... week.'

5 Peter doesn't sing .... well as his brother, but he's a much .... keyboard player.

6 Sally .... come with us tonight .... she's got a cold.

7 I .... learning French five years ...., but I've .... got a lot to learn.

8 I haven't smoked .... ten years. In fact, I can't really remember what a cigarette tastes ....

9 'Is that red Volvo ....?'
   'No, it's .... mine. I .... drive.'

10 I'm .... to get a job in television when I .... university.

11 'How .... does it take to .... to London?'
    'About twenty minutes .... car.'

12 .... was a Bank Holiday yesterday so, as usual, ... were lots of cars on the roads.

13 He's been decorating the kitchen .... last week and still hasn't finished it ....

14 Which bus .... you catch home .... night?

4

15 In Britain, it is .... cheaper to go by bus .... to go by train.

16 .... of them live in Wales but .... one of them speaks Welsh.

17 How .... people .... there at the meeting last night?

18 '...................'s the time, please?'
   'It's .... three o'clock.'

19 'Did you .... anything interesting yesterday?'
   'No, not .... I just .... some shopping in the afternoon, that's
   ....,'

20 You will .... to work much harder .... you're going to pass your
   exam .... the summer.

21 'Have you ever .... to London before?'
   'No, this .... my first visit.'

22 She moved to Belgium two years .... and has been living and working
   .... ever since.

23 We didn't know that our flight .... be delayed. We .... to wait in
   the Departure Lounge for .... than three hours.

24 You .... have seen Mary in London yesterday. She's been in Canada
   .... the past month.

4 Identifying grammatical terms and verb tenses

(a) Which grammatical term can you use to describe the words or phrases in **bold type** in the sentences below? Choose from the following. Look at the example (0).

adjective	......	idiom	......	possessive pronoun	......
adverb of manner	......	indefinite article	......	preposition	......
adverb of frequency	......	interrogative		present participle	......
auxiliary verb	......	pronoun	......	question tag	......
comparative	......	modal verb	......	reflexive pronoun	......
conjunction	......	noun	..0..	time expression	......
definite article	......	personal pronoun	......		
gerund	......	phrasal verb	......		

0 Put the **book** on the table, please.

1 A BMW is **more expensive** than a Fiat.

2 My uncle is **an** accountant.

3 Our team has had a **winning** streak lately.

4 Where were you **the night before last**?

5 You really **ought** to give up smoking.

6 She was wearing a **beautiful** dress.

7 He met his wife **at** a party.

8 We **usually** play tennis at weekends.

9 **Whose** keys are these?

10 Did your son really paint this **himself**?

11 I've decided to **take up** golf.

12 Is this **the** CD you lent me?

13 She couldn't go to the party **because** she was feeling ill.

14 'Whose pen is this?'
'It's **mine**.'

15 Do you like **singing**?

16 He always drives very **carefully**.

17 'I love **you**,' he whispered.

18 My brother **got the sack** last week.

19 He's French, **isn't he**?

20 **Have** you ever met David Brown?

(b) Which verb tenses are shown below? Choose from the following. Again, look at the example (0).

conditional	......	past perfect	......	present perfect	......
future	......	past perfect		present perfect	
future continuous	......	continuous	......	continuous	......
future perfect	......	past simple	..0..	present simple	......
imperative	......	present continuous	......	present simple with	
passive	......	present continuous with		future meaning	......
past continuous	......	future meaning	......		

0 She **wrote** her first novel at the age of nineteen.

1 Fifty people **were killed** in the explosion.

2 He **has been teaching** English as a Foreign Language for ten years.

3 **If it stops** raining soon **we'll go** to the beach.

4 At 8 o'clock last night I **was walking** home through the park.

5 Janet **is having** a party on Saturday.

6 By this time next year they **will have been** married for twenty-five years.

7 The coach **leaves** Swansea at 8.20 and **arrives** at Heathrow at 11.45.

8 **I'll meet** you on Friday outside the station.

9 She was very nervous as she **hadn't flown** before.

10 Just think. This time next week **we'll be lying** on a beach in Bali.

11 I **haven't played** rugby since I left school.

12 We **had been waiting** for nearly forty minutes when the train finally arrived.

13 Jeremy **likes** classical music.

14 It's nearly 7.30. **Wake up** everyone!

15 Peter **is walking** to school.

5 Fill in the verbs

Put the verbs in brackets in the passage below into the correct tenses. There is an example at the beginning (0).

The Car Thief

My cousin and her husband live in Hanwell, one of the suburbs of London. One morning they **(0)** ... (wake up) to find to their dismay that their car **(1)** ... (steal) from outside their house. They immediately **(2)** ... (phone) the police to report the theft, before **(3)** ... (leave) for work by bus.

When they **(4)** ... (return) home later the same day, they **(5)** ... (find) to their surprise that their car **(6)** ... (bring back) and was parked in its usual place outside their house. Under one of the windscreen wipers **(7)** ... (be) a small envelope.

They quickly **(8)** ... (open) it and **(9)** ... (find) a note **(10)** ... (apologize) profusely for 'borrowing' their car. The man who **(11)** ... (write) it explained that he **(12)** ... (not have) a car himself, and his wife **(13)** ... (go) into labour in the middle of the night with their first baby. So he **(14)** ... (hope) they **(15)** ... (not mind) too much that he **(16)** ... (take) their car without their permission in order to run her to the hospital, as it was something of an emergency.

By way of compensation, he **(17)** ... (enclose) two tickets for the West End show *Sunset Boulevard* on Saturday evening. They **(18)** ... (be) both delighted as they loved Andrew Lloyd Webber's music and **(19)** ... (try) for ages to get tickets to this particular musical.

It was a perfect evening. They **(20)** ... (have) front row seats and the show itself was every bit as good as they **(21)** ... (expect). They **(22)** ... (be) in such a good mood after it that they **(23)** ... (decide) to go for a meal at their favourite Italian restaurant. When they eventually **(24)** ... (get) home just after midnight, a new shock **(25)** ... (await) them. While they were away, their house **(26)** ... (burgle)! Everything of value **(27)** ... (steal). They **(28)** ... (know) immediately who the thief was because **(29)** ... (lie) on the kitchen table was a note in handwriting they **(30)** ... (recognize), **(31)** ... (say): HOPE YOU **(32)** ... (enjoy) THE SHOW!

Write your answers here:

0	*woke up*	11		22	
1		12		23	
2		13		24	
3		14		25	
4		15		26	
5		16		27	
6		17		28	
7		18		29	
8		19		30	
9		20		31	
10		21		32	

6 Choose the answer 1: Verbs and adjectives

Read through the sentences below, then decide which answer **a**, **b**, **c** or **d** best fits each space. There is an example at the beginning (0).

0 The best man .... the side of his glass lightly with a knife to get the guests' attention.
   a rapped   b tapped   c hit   d beat

1 The driver .... to avoid hitting the dog.
   a turned   b swerved   c curved   d steered

2 The police .... him for burglary.
   a arrested   b charged   c convicted   d accused

3 Many people .... about the bad behaviour of soccer fans in the town centre after the match.
   a criticized   b disapproved   c complained   d objected

4 I can't wear red. It just doesn't .... me.
   a fit   b suit   c match   d agree with

5 His parents wouldn't .... him stay out later than 10.30 at night.
   a allow   b permit   c agree to   d let

6 The train was .... for several hours because of floods.
   a prevented   b delayed   c detained   d cancelled

7 After a lot of difficulty he finally .... to start the car.
   a succeeded   b coped   c managed   d worked out

8 The manager asked her to .... with the complaint.
   a take care   b attend   c deal   d follow

9 She .... on a banana skin and almost fell down the steps
   a slipped   b stumbled   c tripped   d lost her balance

10 Most library books in the UK are .... using the Dewey decimal system.
   a sorted   b categorized   c graded   d classified

11 Are you .... in applying for the post as assistant manager?
   a keen   b interested   c enthusiastic   d eager

12 My father hates any sort of change. He is very .... in his ways.
   a fixed   b set   c old-fashioned   d stubborn

13 You'll have to speak up. My aunt is very .... of hearing.
   a difficult   b unsure   c hard   d bad

14 'Could you lend me some money till the end of the week?'
   'Sorry, John, I'm a bit .... of cash myself at the moment.'
   a short   b hard up   c scarce   d low

15 My uncle lost his leg in a car accident and now has .... one.
   a a synthetic   b an artificial c a false   d an imitation

16 The police made a .... search of the building after being tipped off that a bomb
   had been planted there.
   a thorough   b conscientious c close   d scrupulous

17 He was two kilos ...., so he decided to go on a diet.
   a fat   b heavy   c too large   d overweight

18 The back door needs oiling. It's very ....
   a shrill   b high-pitched   c squeaky   d creaking

19 I'd better iron this shirt – it's very ....
   a wrinkled   b lined   c squashed   d creased

20 According to statistics, drivers over the age of fifty have .... accidents than
   drivers under twenty-five.
   a smaller   b less   c fewer   d lower

7 Phrasal verbs 1: Break, bring, call

(a) Complete the sentences below with a suitable phrasal verb using *break*. There is an example at the beginning (0).

0 I'm going to have to change my car. It keeps on ...*breaking down*...!

1 The two countries have .... diplomatic relations.

2 Thieves .... at the weekend and stole two valuable paintings.

3 The Second World War .... in 1939.

4 Police were called in to .... the demonstration.

5 The two prisoners .... from their guards and escaped.

(b) Complete the sentences below with a suitable phrasal verb using *bring*.

1 It must have been standing in the pouring rain at Saturday's match that .... your cold.

2 A growing number of people in Britain are calling for the Government to .... the death penalty.

3 It is far more difficult nowadays to .... children than it used to be.

4 Ford have announced that they are going to .... several new models this year.

5 Every time I hear the song *Yesterday* by the Beatles it .... happy memories of my youth.

(c) Complete the sentences below with a suitable phrasal verb using *call*.

1 David said he would .... us at 7.30 to drive us to the station.

2 I tried to .... her .... but the line was engaged.

3 Due to objections from local residents they had to .... the open-air pop concert.

4 If you're visiting Cardiff next month why don't you .... my sister. She'd be delighted to see you again.

5 They .... her Emily .... her grandmother.

(d) Without looking back at exercises a–c, write the correct phrasal verb (*break*, *bring* or *call*) next to the following definitions. (They are in no particular order.)

1 start (e.g. *a war*)   ....

2 collect (someone) (e.g. *by car*)   ....

3 raise (*children*)   ....

4 go and visit (*someone*)   ....

5 to stop working, fail mechanically (e.g. *a car*)   ....

6 be the cause of, lead to (e.g. *a cold*)   ....

7 telephone   ....

8 enter a building illegally, often with force   ....

9 cancel   ....

10 recall, cause a memory to return   ....

8 What's the question?

Write questions next to the following statements to ask about the words in **bold type**. There is an example at the beginning (0).

0 The ring cost **£200,000**.   *How much did the ring cost?*

1 She sees her sister **three times a week**. ....

2 Judy's husband works **in Singapore**. ....

3 Paul weighs **seventy-five kilos.** ....

4 She bought **three pairs of shoes** in the sales. ....

5 David has lived in Brighton **since 1992**. ....

6 They arrested him **for shoplifting**. ....

7 My mother spoke **Welsh** fluently as a child. ....

8 Jill has **bright red** hair. ....

9 This pen once belonged to **Sir Winston Churchill**. ....

10 Jane has **a white MG sports car**. ....

11 He paid for the goods **with a credit card**. ....

12 We play tennis **at least six times** a week. ....

13 She met her boyfriend **at an open-air pop concert**. ....

14 He always has **two boiled eggs** for breakfast. ....

15 We had to wait **over an hour** to get through customs. ....

16 **Peter's** brother is a famous soccer player. ....

17 Cardiff is **about forty miles** from Swansea. ....

18 We finally got home last night **at 11.30**. ....

9 Fill the gaps 1

Fill each of the blank spaces in the sentences below with a suitable word or phrase. There is an example at the beginning (0).

0 '...How much are...... the apples?'
  'Eighty pence a kilo.'

1 If .... Paula at the meeting, remind her to phone me tonight.

2 '.......................... from here to the station?'
  'No, it's only a ten-minute walk.'

3 It's Kevin's party at the weekend. .... to it?

4 According to his instructions, we .... left at the next set of traffic lights.

5 .... harder, you won't pass your exams in the summer.

6 When she first moved to Britain from the States it took her quite a while to .... driving on the left.

7 We'd better leave now because it .... at least half an hour to get there.

8 I'm sorry. I .... you weren't allowed to smoke in here.

9 'I'm at least a kilo overweight.'
  'Then you .... go on a diet.'

10 'How long .... short hair?'
  'Since I joined the army.'

11 'Are you Swedish?'
  'No, ... Norway.'

12 What .... if you won £1 million?

13 That's a nice car. It .... her a lot of money.

14 It might rain later on, so .... an umbrella with you.

15 You .... smoke in here. It's not allowed.

10 Find the mistakes 1

Read the text below and look carefully at each line. Some of the lines are correct, and some have a word which should not be there. If a line is correct put a tick (✓) after it. If a line has a word which should not be there, write down that word. There are two examples at the beginning (0 and 00).

A Thank-You Letter

Dear Chris,

0	I am writing to thank you for the	✓
00	wonderful birthday present you sent for me.	for
1	It was just what I wanted! Molly, she says	....
2	you shouldn't have spent so much of money	....
3	but, like me, she really likes the painting.	....
4	It will looks very nice above the fireplace.	....
5	The birthday party it went off quite well.	....
6	There were about fifteen of us altogether	....
7	that including my parents and Molly's dad.	....
8	We eventually got to the bed at about 2 o'clock	....
9	in the morning! We were really tired.	....
10	When are we going to see you, Alice and the kids	....
11	again? It's been over a year now since then you	....
12	were last here. Why don't you try come down for	....
13	the weekend soon? You know everyone would love	....
14	for to see you again and I know you and I will	....
15	not have lots and lots to talk about!	....
16	Write soon and I look very forward to seeing you again.	....

With best wishes,

Alan

11 Word order

Rearrange the words in the sentences below to form twelve correct questions. (Add commas and capital letters where necessary, and question marks, of course.) There is an example at the beginning (0).

0 the train when last does leave
   When does the last train leave?

1 know Peter Smith do here you works if

2 you way tell station me could to excuse the please me the

3 there day of the is tomorrow chance off having any

4 you how from often borrow do the library books

5 post did I you that you gave remember letter to

6 been country any ever to you Mediterranean Spain have or other

7 your you not with I to toes if me promise step will dance on

8 interested of golf a weekend are round in either of this you playing

9 sometimes is what do about all you life wonder

10 tickets performance are for *Cats* there Saturday's any of left

11 the can on what leave smoke time it and does you bus

12 switch night which the to before of light went you off forgot bed to last you

17

12 Sentence-changing 2

Complete the second sentence so that it has a similar meaning to the first sentence, using the word given. **Do not change the word given**. You must use between two and five words, including the word given. There is an example at the beginning (0).

0 The tea was so hot that we couldn't drink it.
   too
   The tea was ....*too hot to*............ drink.

1 We hired a private nurse to look after my mother when she broke her leg.
   care
   We hired a private nurse .... my mother when she broke her leg.

2 He's only now beginning to recover from his illness.
   get
   It's taken him until .... his illness.

3 David lives quite near the station.
   far
   David .... the station.

4 The programme was so boring that he fell asleep.
   such
   It .... that he fell asleep.

5 My parents don't like us smoking at home.
   approve
   My parents .... smoking at home.

6 We couldn't drive home because of heavy snow.
   prevented
   Heavy snow .... home.

7 Peter wishes now that he hadn't sold his flat.
   regrets
   Peter .... his flat.

8 They say that caviare tastes nice.
   supposed
   Caviare .... nice.

9 It was nearly midnight before everyone left.
   time
   By .... it was nearly midnight.

10 She doesn't find this course very interesting.
    bored
    She .... this course.

11 Did Angela say why she arrived late?
    reason
    Did Angela .... late?

12 She couldn't concentrate because the room was so hot.
    difficult
    The heat in the room .... to concentrate.

13 Question words

Fill in the missing question words below, some of which begin with a preposition. Then choose the correct answer to the question, **a**, **b** or **c**. Write your answers in the boxes at the bottom of the page. There is an example at the beginning (0).

0 ...**When**...... did the first man land on the moon?
   a in 1968   b in 1969   c in 1970

1 .... were the 1960 Olympic Games held?
   a in Rome   b in Tokyo   c in Melbourne

2 .... name was the African state of Namibia formerly known?
   a Rhodesia   b the Congo   c South West Africa

3 .... is Dutch Elm disease so called?
   a because it is only found in Holland
   b because it was first discovered in Holland
   c after the Dutch workers who discovered its cause

4 .... section of the orchestra does the 'tuba' belong?
   a Percussion   b Brass   c Woodwind

5 John F. Kennedy was assassinated in 1963. .... did the letter 'F' in his name stand for?
   a Francis   b Frank   c Fitzgerald

6 ...., in Greek mythology, stole fire from the gods and gave it to mankind?
   a Prometheus   b Theseus   c Achilles

7 .... part of the body would you find 'the bridge'?
   a the ear   b the foot   c the nose

8 .... is the Roman numeral for one thousand?
   a C   b M   c V

9 .... language does the word 'sauna' originate?
   a Swedish   b Norwegian   c Finnish

10 .... legs does a lobster have?
   a 10   b 6   c 8

11 .... composer do you associate *Porgy and Bess* and *Rhapsody in Blue*?

   a Leonard Bernstein   b George Gershwin   c Andrew Lloyd Webber

12 .... face is said to have 'launched a thousand ships'?

   a Joan of Arc's   b Cleopatra's   c Helen of Troy's

13 .... century was the Taj Mahal in India built?

   a 17th   b 16th   c 15th

14 .... must you be before you are allowed to take a normal driving test in the UK?

   a 16   b 18   c 17

15 .... country would you associate with the dish 'couscous'?

   a Greece   b Tunisia   c South Korea

0	1	2	3	4	5	6	7	8	9	10	11	12	13	14	15
b															

14 One word only 2

Read the text below and think of the word which best fits each space. Use only **one** word in each space. There is an example at the beginning (0).

The New Pet

Harry Dawson's two children, Mark and Sarah, were overjoyed **(0)**... he came home one day with a scruffy black and white mongrel **(1)**... the local Dogs' Home. The children **(2)**... to call him 'Lucky'.

A few days **(3)**..., Harry Dawson felt less happy **(4)**... the new family pet when Lucky came **(5)**... the kitchen with a dead rabbit in **(6)**... mouth. The creature was quite fat and well-groomed and was obviously a pet **(7)**... than a wild rabbit.

Sarah **(8)**... one look at it and immediately identified it as **(9)**... to her friend, Cathy Blake, who lived next door **(10)**... one. Fortunately, the Blake family were away **(11)**... holiday in the south of France. So **(12)**... dark that evening, Harry Dawson sneaked into their garden and put the rabbit **(13)**... into the empty hutch*. There were **(14)**... marks on it and he hoped that the Blakes **(15)**... assume it had died **(16)**... natural causes.

A week later, Harry Dawson **(17)**... Mr Blake in the post office and asked him **(18)**... his family was.

'They're very well, thank you,' he said. 'But my daughter, Cathy, is very upset. Her pet rabbit died the week before we went on holiday and **(19)**... really sick person **(20)**... gone and put a dead rabbit in its cage!'

(* a cage for a rabbit and other pets, usually made of wood.)

Write your answers here:

0 .....*when*.....	7	14 ....
1	8	15 ....
2	9	16 ....
3	10	17 ....
4	11	18 ....
5	12	19 ....
6	13	20 ....

15 Prepositions after adjectives

Complete the sentences below with a suitable adjective plus a preposition. Choose from the following. Some of the prepositions will be used more than once.

absent	fond	jealous	satisfied
absorbed	friendly	keen	serious
cruel	good	proud	short
eligible	grateful	responsible	similar
famous	ill	rich	terrified

about	from	of	to
at	in	on	with
for			

1 Both my dogs are very .... ice-cream.

2 I've been .... a cold for over a week.

3 For the last time who is .... this mess?

4 You're not .... leaving this country and going to live in China, are you?

5 I've always been .... water ever since I nearly drowned as a child.

6 Mark's been .... school for over a month. He'll have a lot of catching up to do when he comes back.

7 I'm afraid only single people under the age of thirty are .... membership of this club.

8 Julie's my oldest friend. We've been .... one another since we were at Primary school.

9 Our daughter has just won a scholarship to Cambridge. We are very .... her.

10 Australia is .... natural resources.

11 Could I phone you later, Alan? I'm a bit .... time right now.

12 He was so .... what he was doing that he didn't notice me come into the room.

13 Switzerland is .... its beautiful scenery.

14 My cousin is very .... music and can play four or five instruments.

15 I like ballet but I'm not very .... opera.

16 There's no pleasing our teacher. He's never .... our work!

17 She is .... in character .... her sister.

18 We are .... you for all you've done for us.

19 Michael was .... his brother's success.

20 Small children are often .... animals without realizing it.

16 What's wrong? 1

Only four of the sentences below are grammatically correct. Find these four sentences and rewrite those that contain mistakes. There is an example at the beginning (0).

0 You can't go in there, I'm afraid. They have a meeting.
..You can't go in there, I'm afraid. They are having a meeting...

1 We are much better than they at football.
....

2 At weekends, nearly a thousand visitors to the museum is not uncommon.
....

3 My parents are living in Ireland since 1985.
....

4 He had such a broad Scottish accent that I had difficulty to understand him at first.
....

5 The prize money was shared between the four of them.
....

6 You'd feel a lot better if you would give up smoking.
....

7 Can you tell me where is the post office, please?
....

8 In my opinion, neither of the candidates are really suitable.
....

9 The bananas are my favourite fruit.
....

10 She was having a shower when suddenly the phone rang.
....

11 I've had a tiring day. I think I'll go early to bed tonight.
....

12 They told me that they will arrive on Friday evening.
....

13 The both girls had blonde hair and blue eyes.

....

14 (*end of a letter*) We look forward to hear from you soon.

....

15 No sooner the tennis match started than it began to rain.

....

16 *The Three Musketeers* was written by Alexandre Dumas.

....

17 Of the three sisters, she was the better singer.

....

18 Have you had a lot of rain last week?

....

19 You'll phone as soon as you arrive, won't you?

....

20 David should arrive at 2 o'clock, but he didn't turn up.

....

17 Phrasal verbs 2: Come, cut, fall

(a) Complete the sentences below with a suitable phrasal verb using *come*. There is an example at the beginning (0).

0 I think it's going to be a nice day after all. The sun's just ...._come out_....

1 I .... these old photographs while I was tidying up the attic.

2 It took the boxer over a minute to .... after he had been knocked out by his opponent.

3 'Did Brian win the race?'
'No, he .... second.'

4 She will .... quite a lot of money when her grandmother dies.

5 I don't think much of this new washing powder. Look! The stain on my shirt still hasn't ....!

(b) Complete the sentences below with a suitable phrasal verb using *cut*.

1 I've managed to .... the number of cigarettes I smoke. I just wish I could give it up altogether.

2 Stop doing that, you two! Come on, ... it ....!

3 We were really .... when our cat died. She'd been with us for over ten years and felt like one of the family.

4 During the recession there was little demand for our goods, so we were forced to .... production dramatically.

5 I was phoning my brother when we were suddenly ....

(c) Complete the sentences below with a suitable phrasal verb using *fall*.

1 She slipped and ...., breaking her leg in the process.

2 'I see Paul and Jane aren't speaking to one another.'
'Yes, they've .... again for some reason.'

3 The roof of the building ...., killing two people and injuring twenty others.

4 'Did you get that contract you were talking about?'
'No, it ....'

5 You didn't .... that old pound-note trick, did you? I didn't think you were so gullible!

(d) Without looking back at exercises a–c, write the correct phrasal verb (*come, cut* or *fall*) next to the following definitions. (They are in no particular order.)

1 inherit (*money, property*) ....

2 (be) upset ....

3 fail to materialize, come to nothing
(*e.g. a contract, deal*) ....

4 appear (*e.g. the sun, a flower*) ....

5 be deceived by (*e.g. a false story*) ....

6 find by accident ....

7 reduce consumption (*e.g. cigarettes*) ....

8 disconnect (*telephone*) ....

9 regain consciousness
(*after fainting or being knocked out*) ....

10 quarrel ....

18 Choose the answer 2: Various words

Read through the sentences below, then decide which answer **a**, **b**, **c** or **d** best fits each space. There is an example at the beginning (0).

0 I'm sorry I said that, Mary. It wasn't my ... to hurt you.
   a intention   b purpose   c meaning   d plan

1 Take no ... of him – he's only teasing you!
   a account   b notice   c attention   d regard

2 She had a three-roomed flat in a new residential area on the ... of Copenhagen.
   a border   b suburbs   c outskirts   d near

3 He went to live on the coast for the ... of his health.
   a reason   b sake   c care   d improvement

4 When you buy shares, your investment is always at ... since share prices can go down as well as go up.
   a danger   b trouble   c gamble   d risk

5 You're off to Bangkok, you say? What a ...! So am I.
   a coincidence   b chance   c luck   d fate

6 I wonder if you could give me a ... with the washing-up?
   a help   b assistance   c support   d hand

7 Most of the ... members aboard the new luxury liner were from Pakistan.
   a team   b crew   c gang   d staff

8 My parents were always making ... in public. As a child I found it very embarrassing.
   a quarrels   b arguments   c scenes   d fuss

9 The Queen has no real power. She's just a ....
   a figurehead   b mascot   c sleeping partner   d puppet

10 The child was throwing stones at the pigeons but his mother didn't take any ... of him.
   a attention   b notice   c control   d regard

11 Take an umbrella with you ... it rains.
   a in case   b even though   c despite   d because

12 We're going to miss this train ... we hurry up.
   a provided   b if   c in spite of   d unless

13 He went to live in France for a year ... he could pick up the language.
   a because of   b in order   c so that   d therefore

14 Everyone's been invited to the party ... for Cathy.
   a except   b apart   c but   d with the exception

15 ... than paying out all that money for a hotel, why don't you come and stay with
   us instead? We've got lots of room.
   a Instead   b Better   c Rather   d In preference

16 In ... women live longer than men in most countries.
   a average   b the whole   c reality   d general

17 There was a large notice in the hotel corridor saying: '... fire, press the alarm bell'.
   a If   b On account of c In case of   d Supposing

18 Who else went with you to the concert ... David and Jean?
   a apart   b besides   c except   d beside

19 People in Wales are ... Labour supporters.
   a most   b all in all   c entire   d predominantly

20 At the age of fifty, he finally admitted to himself that it was ... unlikely that he was
   going to be a pop idol.
   a greatly   b largely   c highly   d fully

19 Sentence-changing 3

Complete the second sentence so that it has a similar meaning to the first sentence, using the word given. **Do not change the word given**. You must use between two and five words, including the word given. There is an example at the beginning (0).

0 'Will you lend me five pounds?' he asked.
borrow
He asked *to borrow / if he could borrow* five pounds.

1 We started eating when all the guests had arrived.
until
We .... all the guests had arrived.

2 I should very much like to play the guitar.
wish
I .... play the guitar.

3 The pop star left by the back exit so as to avoid meeting the press.
order
The pop star left by the back exit .... the press.

4 Our driving laws and theirs are not the same.
different
Our driving laws .... theirs.

5 Sally hasn't contacted me for over six weeks.
heard
I .... over six weeks ago.

6 'You really must stay the night,' he said to us.
insisted
He .... the night.

7 They make 2,000 cars a week at that factory.
turns
That factory .... 2,000 cars a week.

8 He was punished for his bad behaviour.
badly
If he ...., he wouldn't have been punished.

9 Speaking personally, I don't care whether she comes with us or not.
matter
It .... whether she comes with us or not.

10 I don't really want to go out tonight.
prefer
I .... go out tonight.

11 'Would you like to play tennis on Friday?' Emily asked Nick.
felt
Emily asked Nick .... tennis on Friday.

12 As soon as he came in, he switched on the television.
immediately
He came in .... the television.

20 What's missing? 1

Read the text below and look carefully at each line. Some of the lines are correct, and some have a word missing. If a line is correct put a tick (✓) after it. If a line has a missing word, use a stroke (/) to show where a word has been left out, and on the right suggest what the missing word might be. There are two examples at the beginning (0 and 00).

An Embarrassing Moment

0	It happens to everyone sooner or later, that	✓
00	dreaded moment when you say or do / that makes	*something*
1	you so embarrassed that you wish a big hole	....
2	appear in the ground down which you could	....
3	disappear. One of most embarrassing moments	....
4	happened when I was just twenty-two and living	....
5	in Eastbourne. I gone for an interview for a job	....
6	as receptionist in a large hotel in Brighton.	....
7	I had driven there and, because of the traffic	....
8	and the difficulty finding the hotel, I was	....
9	slightly late. I had just reached the hotel car and	....
10	was about to reverse into a parking space a man	....
11	in a big, white Jaguar car drove into it. This made	....
12	me really so I wound down the window and	....
13	shouted and swore him. But he just ignored me	....
14	and walked away, of course made me even	....
15	madder. To add to my difficulties, it was summer	....
16	the car park was full so I had to wait another five	....
17	minutes or so before I find an empty parking	....

18 space. This time I was over a quarter of an hour ....

19 late for the interview, so I rushed to the ....

20 manager's office, knocked the door and walked in. ....

21 The manager was a man was sitting behind his ....

22 desk. When he looked up I died – it was the same ....

23 man that I had shouted and sworn at the car ....

24 park – the one who had taken my parking space! ....

25 Happily, we both saw funny side of things and I ....

26 ended up the job, but only on one condition – that ....

27 I promised to shout and swear at the guests! ....

21 Word-building 1

Use the word given in capitals at the end of each sentence to form a noun that fits in the space. There is an example at the beginning (0).

0 Which ....*artist*.... do you prefer – Monet or Picasso?   ART

1 How much did they charge for .... to the   ADMIT
  Van Gogh exhibition?

2 The reporter asked the Prime Minister for   ANALYSE
  his .... of the situation.

3 She wasn't feeling very well, so she made   APPOINT
  an .... to see the doctor.

4 Scotland is well known for the .... of its scenery.   BEAUTIFUL

5 My wife and I are always having .... about   ARGUE
  whose turn it is to do the vacuuming.

6 He'll never get the job; he lacks .... in himself.   CONFIDENT

7 Scandinavian Airways apologized for any ....   CONVENIENT
  caused by the late arrival of flight SK 506.

8 Cinema or theatre? It's your .... I really   DECIDE
  don't mind where we go.

9 To his great ...., he failed to get a place at   DISAPPOINT
  university.

10 I seem to spend most of my time at work dealing with   INQUIRE
  .... from the public.

11 He could give no satisfactory .... for his   EXPLAIN
  behaviour.

12 Burglaries seem to occur in this area with   FREQUENT
  alarming ....

13 'Life has not been easy for you,' began the fortune-teller.   HAPPY
  'There seems to be a lot of .... in your past.'

14 The one thing you need above all else to be a   IMAGINE
   successful writer is a vivid ....

15 The job requires a working .... of French   KNOW
   and German.

16 My brother's ambition is to be a professional ....   MUSIC

17 Is there any .... of us all getting together again   POSSIBLE
   on Friday?

18 It was your own .... and nothing else that led   STUPID
   to the accident!

19 There can be little doubt that .... in modern   VIOLENT
   society is on the increase.

20 They greeted us with such .... that we felt   WARM
   immediately at home.

22 Infinitive or -ing form?

Complete the sentences below with a suitable verb, using either the infinitive (*to buy,* *to come,* etc.) or the -ing form (*buying, coming,* etc.). Choose from the following and use each verb once only. There are two examples at the beginning (0 and 00).

be	hurt	pass	stay	think
buy	leave	play	take	walk
come	like	save	talk	want
get	live	see	teach	win
give	meet			

0   Remember ...*to buy*.... some milk on your way home tonight.

00   I'm busy at the moment. Would you mind ..*coming*... back later?

1   I'm sorry, Joe. I didn't mean .... your feelings.

2   When she was a child, her parents wouldn't allow her .... in the street.

3   There must be something wrong with Simon. He keeps .... he's being followed by MI5.

4   As they'd received a bomb threat, the police ordered everyone .... the building.

5   What with inflation and everything, it's just not worth .... nowadays.

6   I remember .... to be a pop star when I was a child.

7   Don't pretend .... jazz. I know you hate it really.

8   'Mary hasn't got a car. Would you mind .... her a lift?'

   'No, not at all.'

9   I really enjoy going to parties and .... new people.

10   Her parents were very strict and wouldn't allow her .... out later than 10.30 at night.

11 Parents usually warn their children against .... to strangers.

12 I never go swimming because I dislike .... my hair wet.

13 I agreed .... her English if she helped me with my Spanish.

14 It was a very tough match, but in the end England managed .... by two goals to one.

15 He suggested .... a taxi to the station.

16 The film star disguised herself to avoid .... recognized.

17 Would you dare .... through a graveyard on your own at night?

18 She was very upset when she failed .... her driving test.

19 He wasn't happy with his room so he demanded .... the manager.

20 It's hard to imagine .... without television, isn't it? What on earth would you do in the evenings?

23 Some or any combinations

Complete the following sentences using *some* or *any* or words beginning with *some* and *any* (*something, anyone*, etc.).

1 'Who were you talking to?'
  'Oh, it wasn't .... you know.'

2 My uncle has so much money. I wish he'd give me .... as I never seem to have ....

3 '....................'s been reading my mail!'
  'Well, don't look at me. I haven't been .... near the office all day!'

4 '.................... to declare, Sir?'
  'Well, I bought ....perfume for my wife, but they told me in the shop I wouldn't have to pay .... duty on it.'

5 Why don't you bring .... of your friends to the party? Unless you're doing .... else of course.

6 Most people don't have .... idea of how serious the present economic crisis is. If the Government don't do .... soon to bring down unemployment then they're not going to have .... choice but to put taxes up again.

7 'But there must be .... biscuits left! I bought a whole packet yesterday.'
  '.................... must have eaten them, because there definitely aren't .... left in the tin.'

8 'I feel like going out .... this weekend.'
  '.................... in particular?'
  'No, not really. I just need to do .... different for a change.'

9 'Did you go .... last night?'
  'No, we had .... friends round for a meal.'

10 'Can I help you?'
  'Yes, I'd like .... information about trains to Leeds, please. Are there .... early in the morning?'

11 We haven't got .... milk. Pop out and get ...., would you, please?

12 These, without .... doubt, are .... of the biggest pumpkins I have ever seen. They should definitely win first prize in the Garden Show.

24 One word only 3

Read the text below and think of the word which best fits each space. Use only **one** word in each space. There is an example at the beginning (0).

The Hitchhiker

It was a very wet and windy day and David Williams was **(0)**... to the skin **(1)**.... he stood at the side of the road **(2)**... to hitch a lift. **(3)**... far, only four cars had **(4)**... along and each one had gone past **(5)**... stopping. David was beginning to wonder if anyone **(6)**... stop for him when a lorry suddenly **(7)**... up and the driver told him to hop on the back as there wasn't **(8)**... in the cab. David accepted gladly and quickly climbed aboard.

To his **(9)**..., in the back was an empty coffin. **(10)**... it was still raining heavily, David decided to climb **(11)**... it for shelter. Standing by the roadside had **(12)**... him feel very tired, so it wasn't **(13)**... before he had fallen fast asleep.

While he was sleeping, the lorry **(14)**... stopped again to **(15)**... up another hitch-hiker. Like David, he too climbed on to the back of the lorry. By now, the rain had stopped and the sun had come **(16)**.... It began to **(17)**... very hot inside the coffin and David suddenly woke up. Without thinking, he lifted the lid **(18)**... the coffin, saw the stranger sitting there and shouted: 'Have I **(19)**... asleep for long?'

His fellow hitchhiker took one look at David, screamed **(20)**... fear and jumped **(21)**... the lorry in panic. Needless to say, he has never hitchhiked **(22)**....

Write your answers here:

0 ...*soaked*...	8	16 ....
1	9	17 ....
2	10	18 ....
3	11	19 ....
4	12	20 ....
5	13	21 ....
6	14	22 ....
7	15	

25 Prepositions after verbs

Complete the sentences below with a suitable verb plus a preposition. Choose from the following and make any necessary changes. Some of the prepositions will be used more than once.

apologize	compliment	protect	succeed
arrive	feel sorry	rely	suffer
believe	insure	remind	think
care	lose	share	translate
charge	prefer	smell	write

about	by	in	on
against	for	into	to
among	from	of	with
at			

1 You should always .... your home .... fire.

2 'Does Peter .... you .... Michael Jackson?'
  'No, he doesn't look anything like him.'

3 If I were you Julie I'd .... very carefully .... his offer. I don't think you'll get a better one.

4 She made the children .... their bad behaviour at the party.

5 The man was arrested and .... murder.

6 Don't forget to wear a scarf. It will .... you .... the cold.

7 After three attempts she finally .... breaking the world record.

8 *Hamlet* was .... Shakespeare.

9 'Does Mark really .... flying saucers?'
  'Oh yes, he's quite convinced they exist.'

10 The mother told the group of children to .... the sweets .... themselves.

11 She felt really pleased when her teacher .... her .... her homework.

12 It was largely my fault that we .... tennis. I played so badly.

13 We left Heathrow airport at 16.45 and .... Copenhagen at 19.30.

14 Although she had only painted the kitchen, the whole flat .... paint.

15 My sister .... hay fever every summer.

16 I really .... people who are tone deaf. It must be awful not to be able to sing.

17 'Would you .... another piece of cake, Frank?
'No thanks, Jill. I really couldn't eat another thing.'

18 Most young people .... pop music .... classical music.

19 Ask Mike to do it. You can .... him. He never lets you down.

20 This book has been .... five languages, including Russian.

26 Sentence-changing 4

Complete the second sentence so that it has a similar meaning to the first sentence, using the word given. **Do not change the word given.** You must use between two and five words, including the word given. There is an example at the beginning (0).

0 Paul likes music.
interested
Paul ...*is interested in*..... music.

1 Do you want a sandwich?
care

....
a sandwich?

2 Is this pen yours?
belong
Does .... you?

3 David was too ill to go camping with us.
enough
David ....
to go camping with us.

4 You can't vote unless you are over eighteen.
must
You ....
to vote.

5 I think we should go home now.
time
It ....
home now.

6 I certainly won't go there again!
last
That ....
I go there!

7 I regret not getting married.
wish
I .... married.

8 He found it hard to start the car.
difficulty
He .... the car.

9 Why wouldn't she give you her telephone number?
refuse
Why .... give you her telephone number?

10 John and I last quarrelled over a week ago.
fallen
John and I ....
for over a week.

11 I doubt very much that you saw Carla at the party as she's in Scotland at the moment.
can't
You .... Carla at the party as she's in Scotland at the moment.

12 After nearly an hour the coach had still not arrived.
sign
After nearly an hour ....
.... of the coach.

27 Phrasal verbs 3: Get, go, keep

(a) Complete the sentences below with a suitable phrasal verb using *get*. There is an example at the beginning (0).

0 I ....*get on*.......... really well with my mother-in-law. In fact, I prefer her to my own mother.

1 'When did you .... from your holidays?'
'Last Friday.'

2 The burglar .... through an open bedroom window.

3 The plug was behind the bookcase which made it very difficult to ....
....

4 I tried phoning twice but couldn't .... The line was engaged each time.

5 All this rain is really .... me .... I wish it were summer again.

(b) Complete the sentences below with a suitable phrasal verb using *go*.

1 After months of negotiations, the deal finally ....

2 Time always seems to .... so quickly when you're enjoying yourself.

3 Don't eat that cheese – it's ....!

4 Do you think this tie will .... my yellow jacket?

5 There was a loud explosion. Seconds later all the lights ....

(c) Complete the sentences below with a suitable phrasal verb using *keep*.

1 Try to .... the subject of politics tonight. We don't want Peter and Colin quarrelling again, do we?

2 They were walking so quickly that she found it hard to .... them. (*three words needed*)

3 Do you have any sprays or anything else that will .... flies and mosquitoes?

4 I know you haven't found a job yet, but you've got to .... trying. You mustn't give up.

5 You haven't told me everything, have you? You're still .... something ....

(d) Without looking back at exercises a–c, write the correct phrasal verb (*get, go* or *keep*) next to the following definitions. (They are in no particular order.)

1 be connected (*by telephone*)   ....

2 match (*style, colour*)   ....

3 maintain same speed level as others   ....

4 have a good relationship with someone   ....

5 stop burning (*e.g. a light, candle*)   ....

6 return (*e.g. from a holiday*)   ....

7 withhold (*information*)   ....

8 go bad (*food, milk*)   ....

9 depress, demoralize   ....

10 pass (*time*)   ....

28 Find the mistakes 2

Read the text below and look carefully at each line. Some of the lines are correct, and some have a word which should not be there. If a line is correct put a tick (✓) after it. If a line has a word which should not be there, write down that word. There are two examples at the beginning (0 and 00).

A Meal To Remember

0 A German couple who went to the Hong Kong .... the ....

00 for a holiday have returned without their pet .... ✓ ....

1 poodle, Greta, following after a very traumatic ....

2 experience in a Chinese restaurant there. ....

3 They were out dining one evening and, as so ....

4 usual, had their pet poodle with them. Just ....

5 after when they had ordered their meal the dog ....

6 started to whine, so that they asked a waiter ....

7 come over to their table and pointed to the ....

8 poodle while they made an eating motions to ....

9 show they wanted it to be fed. ....

10 Eventually as the waiter appeared to understand ....

11 and took Greta off into the kitchen. About after ....

12 an hour later he came back with their main dish ....

13 and when they picked up inside the silver lid they ....

14 found out their poodle roasted inside, garnished ....

15 with pepper, sauce and bamboo shoots. The ....

16 couple, suffering from emotional shock, have ....

17 decided for to return to Hamburg immediately. ....

29 Fill the gaps 2

Fill each of the blank spaces in the sentences below with a suitable word or phrase. There is an example at the beginning (0).

0 ..*Even though/Although*.. he was nearly seventy, he could still beat me at tennis.

1 You're late! You .... here half an hour ago.

2 Even if we had run all the way we still .... catch the train.

3 'Cigarette?'
'No, thank you. I .... two years ago.'

4 Do you really .... so soon? Can't you stay just a little bit longer?

5 Sorry everyone, I'm going to have to go to bed. I'm just .... staying up late.

6 My neighbour is .... people you could ever wish to meet.

7 Don't park there .... get a parking ticket.

8 'Another cup of coffee?'
'No, thanks. I .... two cups already.'

9 Even if we'd caught a taxi, we still .... there in time.

10 The weather was so bad that they decided .... the barbecue.

11 'What .... a living?'
'She's an accountant.'

12 I was only eighteen when I started working for Brown & Company. So by June next year I .... for them for forty-five years.

13 What's happened to Jake? I .... him since 1990.

14 The holiday was a total disaster. I just wish .... somewhere else.

15 My wife was staying with her mother in Scotland last weekend, so you .... have seen her in London.

16 When she broke her leg, it was nearly a year .... walk properly again.

17 I'm sorry you .... to Majorca with us. It really won't be the same without you.

18 Give me a call .... you arrive.

19 I hope David's all right. .... over three weeks since we last heard from him.

20 I .... go there by air than by boat.

21 If we had hurried up we .... missed the train.

22 Could you give .... tomorrow afternoon? My number is 842035.

23 .... leave the building immediately, I shall call the police!

24 It was not until .... her glasses off that I recognized her.

25 How often .... books from the library?

30 What's missing? 2

Read the text below and look carefully at each line. Some of the lines are correct, and some have a word missing. If a line is correct put a tick (✓) after it. If a line has a missing word, use a stroke (/) to show where a word has been left out and on the right suggest what the missing word might be. There are two examples at the beginning (0 and 00).

The Lady Vanishes

0	In 1889 an Englishwoman and her daughter, on a	✓
00	visit to / Great Exhibition in Paris, checked into one	the
1	of the most expensive hotels there. Each had her	....
2	room. The daughter wanted to take in sights and	....
3	sounds of the city immediately but her mother, tired	....
4	after the trip, wanted to sleep. The girl accordingly	....
5	went out alone, strolled the Champs Elysées	....
6	saw the Eiffel Tower.	....
7	She returned to her mother's room six hours later,	....
8	she found it empty. There was no sign of her mother	....
9	ever been there. When she checked with the manager	....
10	he insisted that no one at the hotel had seen her or	....
11	mother check in. The mother had disappeared!	....
12	The desperate girl searched for weeks before finally	....
13	returning to England. She died several years in a	....
14	mental hospital, having got over 'losing' her mother.	....
15	So what was the explanation? The daughter had	....
16	gone sightseeing, her mother complained to the hotel	....
17	doctor she felt ill. She had contracted the plague!	....
18	The hotel officials were instructed to say a word to	....
19	anyone about this, in case visitors the city and the	....
20	Great Exhibition ended in disaster. The mother's	....
21	room was quickly redecorated and couple moved in.	....
22	No one knows what happened the mother.	....

31 Broken sentences 1 (*if-clauses*)

(a) Complete the clauses 1–16 with a suitable clause from those marked a–p. Write your answers in the boxes on the next page.

1 She'll have to wait in my room

2 I'll have to sell my car

3 You'd feel a lot better

4 We would have caught the last bus

5 You'll lose quite a lot of weight

6 He'll probably pass his exams

7 She won't be able to go to university

8 We would have had a picnic this afternoon

9 I'd ask her to marry me

10 He told us he wouldn't go on working

11 You'll fail your exams

12 The firm wouldn't have gone bankrupt

13 I'll drive you to the station

14 I'd lend you the money

15 You'd make a better impression at the interview

16 The match will go to extra time

a unless she passes her school exams.

b if I wasn't so broke myself.

c unless one of the teams scores soon.

d if he keeps on working hard.

e if you cut your hair and wore a suit.

f if I thought she'd say yes.

g if you gave up smoking.

h if I can borrow Mum's car.

i unless you work harder.

j if you go jogging every day.

k unless I get a job soon.

l if they hadn't tried to expand so quickly.

m if it hadn't rained.

n if we hadn't stayed for another drink.

o if he won a lot of money.

p if she arrives before I get back from lunch.

1	2	3	4	5	6	7	8	9	10	11	12	13	14	15	16

(b) Now complete the sentences below using the correct tense of the verbs in brackets. Add any other words that may be necessary.

1 We will have to cancel the concert tomorrow if it .... (*rain*)

2 You .... weight if you ate fewer cream cakes. (*lose*)

3 I .... the job if I had known it was going to be so badly paid. (*not take*)

4 If I lend you the money, ... me back by the end of next week? (*pay*)

5 If you had been more careful the accident .... (*not happen*)

6 He .... with us unless his brother comes too. (*not come*)

7 If you .... harder you would soon be able to play the guitar well. (*practise*)

8 She .... the match unless she plays better. (*lose*)

9 If the driver .... in time; the dog would probably have been killed. (*not brake*)

10 You wouldn't have failed your exam if you .... harder. (*work*)

32 Choose the answer 3

Read the text below and decide which word **a**, **b**, **c** or **d** best fits each space. There is an example at the beginning (0).

A Lucky Escape

It was November 1971 in London on a day **(0)**... any other. On one of the city's underground stations, a train **(1)**... the platform. Suddenly, a young man **(2)**... himself **(3)**... into the path of the moving train. The horrified driver slammed on the brakes, certain that there was no way to stop the train **(4)**... the man was crushed **(5)**... the wheels. But miraculously the train did stop. The first carriage **(6)**... be jacked up to **(7)**... the badly injured man, but the wheels had not passed over him and he **(8)**....

The young man **(9)**... out to be a gifted architect who was recovering **(10)**... a nervous breakdown. His amazing rescue from death was **(11)**... coincidence. For the **(12)**... of the accident revealed that the train had not stopped **(13)**... the driver's hasty breaking. Seconds before, acting **(14)**... impulse and completely **(15)**... of the man about to throw himself on the tracks, a passenger had **(16)**... down the emergency handle, which automatically applies the brakes of the train. The passenger had no **(17)**... reason for doing so. In fact, the Transport Authority considered prosecuting him on the **(18)**... that he had no reasonable cause for using the emergency system!

0 a as	b like	c by	d similar
1 a has reached	b entered	c was approaching	d had got to
2 a leapt	b plunged	c pushed	d hurled
3 a directly	b fully	c sudden	d at once
4 a while	b until	c before	d as
5 a through	b under	c with	d behind
6 a must	b had to	c would have to	d should
7 a repair	b take back	c remove	d liberate

8 a survived   b perished   c succeeded   d relived

9 a came   b made   c proved   d turned

10 a over   b of   c from   d by

11 a because   b depending on   c with a view to d based on

12 a investigation b inquiry   c conclusion   d examination

13 a despite   b until   c during   d because of

14 a with   b by   c on   d with

15 a unknown   b unaware   c unconnected   d unsure

16 a held   b broken   c pulled   d thrown

17 a specialist   b peculiar   c convinced   d particular

18 a reason   b grounds   c cause   d motive

33 Choose the caption

Which captions best illustrate the drawings below? Choose from the following and write your answers in the boxes below.

a He's stopped smoking.
b He's stopped to smoke.
c Pass me a knife, please.
d Pass me the knife, please.
e She's used to skating.
f She used to skate.
g He's having his hair cut.
h He's cutting his hair.
i The man is boring.
j The man is bored.

34 Missing words in a text

Read through the following newspaper article and then choose the best phrase given below to fill each of the gaps. Write one letter (a–p). Not all the phrases will be used.

Smoking 'will kill one million young people'

PROLONGED smoking will kill around one million British teenagers and children in middle age (1)..............., says a report published yesterday.

A further one million will die of tobacco-related diseases in old age, (2).............. at the Imperial Cancer Research Fund and the World Health Organization. On present trends, 4–5 million young Britons (3)...............

Professor Richard Peto, of the ICRF, said that worldwide somebody (4).............. which was already killing three million people each year, and the number was increasing.

'In most countries (5)............... If current smoking patterns persist, then by the time the young smokers of today (6).............. there will be about ten million deaths a year from tobacco – one every three seconds. Furthermore, young people continue to see misleading portrayals (7)............... It tells them that lighting up is acceptable. It is no surprise therefore that 90 per cent of smokers start when young.'

He argued that (8).............. about the effects of prolonged smoking, because of the very long delay between cause and effect. The risk came decades later.

'If cigarette smokers start young and don't stop, about half will be killed by tobacco.' This means that the developing countries (9).............., said Professor Peto.

Dr Alan Lopez of the World Health Organization in Geneva, added: 'The WHO has called on governments everywhere to protect children from (10)............... The sooner tobacco advertising is banned, the more lives will be saved.'

Professor Sir Richard Doll – one of the two people (11).............. forty years ago – urged the Government to increase tax on cigarettes and ban advertising.

It is quite incredible they don't do it. Here you have something that (12).............. and people are being encouraged to do it. It is immoral, there is no other word for it.'

56

a of smoking as romantic and sporting

b who proved the link between smoking and lung cancer

c there has been widespread misunderstanding

d there has been little notice paid

e if current patterns continue

f is killing one sixth of the population prematurely

g are sitting on a time bomb

h the worst is yet to come

i it is both cruel and deadly

j according to the report by scientists

k the advertising and promotion of tobacco

l died every ten seconds through smoking

m will probably kill millions of young people

n reach middle or old age

o will become regular smokers

p refusal to ban tobacco advertising

35 Prepositional phrases

(a) Here are 30 words and phrases in alphabetical order. Put them under the correct preposition. Some of them can be used with more than one preposition.

a change	ever	last	sale
a diet	fire	mistake	sight
a hurry	first	night	the moment
air	heart	once	the ordinary
all means	hire	order	trouble
breath	holiday	particular	work
business	hospital	private	
date	instance	purpose	

AT	BY	FOR

IN	ON	OUT OF

(b) Now complete the following sentences with a suitable prepositional phrase. Choose from the ones in (a). There is an example at the beginning (0).

0 Owls usually hunt ...*at night*... They can see really well in the dark.

1 'May I join you?'
   'Yes, ...'

2 'Are you going to Spain for a holiday?'
   'No, I'll be there ....'

3 I've put on nearly three kilos. I think I'd better go ....

4 I know her ...., but I've no idea what she's called.

5 My uncle had a stroke last week and has been .... ever since.

6 After running for the bus I was ....

7 The people at number 10 are emigrating to Australia, so they've put their house up ....

8 Sorry, Nick, I can't stop. I'm .... this morning. But I'll phone you later on.

9 Let's go out for a meal tonight .... I'm fed up with cooking.

10 Mr Grant's very busy .... Could you come back later?

11 When you saw her on TV she seemed such a nice, kind person, but .... she was vicious and cruel – especially towards her children.

12 Our teacher made us learn the words of the poem ....

13 It was an accident I tell you. I certainly didn't drop the vase ....

14 We'll have to use the stairs. The lift is ....

15 'My darling, I will love you ....!' he promised.

16 I didn't recognize him .... because he had grown a beard since I last saw him.

36 Sentence-changing 5

Complete the second sentence so that it has a similar meaning to the first sentence, using the word given. **Do not change the word given**. You must use between two and five words, including the word given. There is an example at the beginning (0).

0 'What's the date today?' Michael asked.
know
Michael *wanted to know what* the date was today.

1 Their wedding takes place on Saturday.
married
They .... on Saturday.

2 Would you like some more sauce with your meat?
enough
Have .... with your meat?

3 How likely is she to win the race?
chances
What .... the race?

4 He wished he had gone to university.
regretted
He .... gone to university.

5 Paul had difficulty in starting the car.
difficult
Paul .... the car.

6 Take a jumper with you because it might get cold later on.
case
Take a jumper with you ....
.... cold later on.

7 How much did that jacket cost?
pay
How much ....
that jacket?

8 The only question I had wrong was question seven.
except
I had .... question seven.

9 I don't think I'll go to Jane's party on Saturday.
doubt
I .... to Jane's party on Saturday.

10 It was very kind of them to help us.
grateful
We .... for their help.

11 My uncle had never been abroad before.
trip
It was .... abroad.

12 This is the best food I've ever eaten.
better
I've .... this.

60

37 Word-building 2

Use the word given in capitals at the end of each sentence to form an adjective that fits in the space. There is an example at the beginning (0).

0 Cornwall has lots of ....*beautiful*.... beaches. **BEAUTY**

1 She was very .... and aimed to be Prime Minister one day. **AMBITION**

2 The tennis player was so ...., with himself at losing the match that he smashed his racket into the net and stormed off the court. **ANGER**

3 I'm not surprised that she's so .... After all, her father's a musician and her mother's an actress. **ART**

4 Ted's such a .... driver, isn't he? I really can't understand how he hasn't had an accident yet. **CARE**

5 To survive today, a company needs to be very .... **COMPETE**

6 Amanda's farewell party before she emigrated to New Zealand was a very .... occasion. **EMOTION**

7 Do you think boys are more .... than girls? **ENERGY**

8 'I hope you had an .... evening at the theatre.' 'Yes, we had a wonderful time, thank you.' **ENJOY**

9 He took the computer back to the shop because it was .... **FAULT**

10 I kept well away from the dog because it looked rather .... **FRIEND**

11 Being on board a car ferry when a fire broke out was one of the most .... experiences of my life. **FRIGHT**

12 Children who start smoking don't usually realize how .... the habit is. **HARM**

13 There are still far too many hungry and ....   HOME
people in our large cities.

14 Be careful how you drive. The roads are very   ICE
.... tonight.

15 Most people feel very .... before   NERVE
making a speech.

16 The pop concert was so .... that we   NOISE
left after half an hour.

17 It was very .... of you to expect everyone   REASON
to work overtime tonight at such short notice.

18 Don't ask Paul to do it. He's so ....   RELY
You just can't trust him.

19 He was very .... with the way he had   SATISFY
played. Both he and his coach knew he should
have played a lot better.

20 Be careful with that microscope – it's a very   SENSE
.... instrument.

21 How could you say that to her? You ought to   SHAME
be .... of yourself!

22 I couldn't help feeling .... when he   SUSPECT
offered me £250 to help him carry his bags
through customs.

23 If you overcook vegetables they lose all their   TASTE
flavour and become completely ....

24 If you're thinking of going to work abroad,   USE
there are some very .... addresses at
the back of this book.

25 I hate PVC windows and doors. I much prefer   WOOD
.... ones.

38 Phrasal verbs 4: Look, put, take

(a) Complete the sentences below with a suitable phrasal verb using *look*. There is an example at the beginning (0).

0 Could you ...... *look after* ...... the children for me on Friday evening? I've got to go to a Parent–Teacher Association meeting.

1 ....! There's a car coming.

2 Most children .... the summer holidays. (*three words needed*)

3 I often .... the sixties. They were such great times and I was so happy then. (*three words needed*)

4 If you don't know the meaning of a word, ... it .... in a dictionary.

5 We've had several complaints from customers this week, Mrs Baker. I'd like you to .... them please.

(b) Complete the sentences below with a suitable phrasal verb using *put*.

1 The fire brigade arrived quickly and soon .... the fire.

2 We've decided to get rid of our coal fires and .... central heating instead.

3 He tried to .... some money each week in case of emergencies.

4 By the way, James, there's no meeting tonight after all. It's been .... until next week.

5 Their dog was old and obviously in pain. So they decided to have it ....

(c) Complete the sentences below with a suitable phrasal verb using *take*.

1 'Your daughter has a very good voice, Mr Blake.'
  'Well, she .... her mother, not me. I can't sing a note.'

2 If you want a job, Julie, Woolworths are .... extra staff for Christmas.

3 I tried playing golf once but never really .... it. As far as I was concerned it was nothing more than a good walk spoilt.

4 He sounded so convincing when he said he was a film director that we were all completely .... You can imagine how surprised we were to learn that in reality he was an out-of-work plumber.

5 There's a rumour going round that Sony are planning to .... a top American computer company.

(d) Without looking back at exercises a–c, write the correct phrasal verb (*look, put* or *take*) next to the following definitions. (They are in no particular order.)

1 examine, investigate (e.g. *a complaint*)   ....

2 develop a liking for (*something*)   ....

3 save (*money*)   ....

4 try to find (*information*)   ....

5 extinguish (*a fire*)   ....

6 gain control of a company   ....

7 kill humanely (*a pet*)   ....

8 take care of, care for (*someone*)   ....

9 resemble (*in looks, talent*)   ....

10 remember the past   ....

39 More than one meaning

The following newspaper extracts, headlines, etc. are written in such a way that there is an extra, unexpected meaning to the one that was intended – often with amusing results. Explain the 'other' meaning and then try rewriting numbers 1, 3, 4, 6, 7, 9, 10, and 12 so that they only have the intended meanings. There is an example at the beginning (0).

0 Dear milkman, Baby arrived yesterday. Please leave another.
 'Unexpected' meaning: Please leave another baby

 Can be rewritten as:
 Dear milkman, Baby arrived yesterday. Please leave another pint of milk.

1 It is bad manners to break your bread and roll in your soup.

2 WANTED: zinc bath for adult with strong bottom.

3 The motorist involved in the accident declared that the other driver smelled of drink. So did a policeman.

4 ANGRY BULL INJURES FARMER WITH A GUN

5 Dog for sale: eats anything and is very fond of children.

6 West End Theatre is looking for actors and actresses to perform in a play dealing with the effects of drugs. Experience preferred.

7 WANTED: a reliable young woman to wash, iron and milk two cows.

8 For a moment he stood there looking into her eyes. Between them was a bowl of daffodils.

9 Busy seaside restaurant requires man to wash dishes and two waitresses.

10 The Queen named the ship as she slid gently into the water.

11 FOR SALE: electric saw by a Manchester man with newly sharpened teeth.

12 If your baby does not thrive on raw milk, boil it.

40 Broken sentences 2 (*conjunctions*)

(a) Complete the clauses 1–16 with a suitable clause from those marked a–p. Write your answers in the boxes on the next page.

1 It was so hot

2 He promised to give his parents a call

3 I wouldn't take a job there

4 As a child, she wasn't allowed to go to bed

5 You can borrow the car

6 He never went abroad on holiday

7 We'll have a picnic this afternoon

8 Take a jumper with you

9 I always feel like singing

10 Everyone in the room went completely quiet

11 She couldn't go to the party

12 She'll be a very good reporter

13 She confessed that she married her husband

14 I won't pass my exams in the summer

15 Stevie Wonder is a brilliant musician

16 I'll go to the party with you tonight

a even if they offered me £5,000 a month.

b once she's had more experience.

c whenever I hear that song on the radio.

d even though she didn't love him at the time.

e in spite of being blind.

f because she was ill.

g until she had kissed everyone goodnight.

h as the headmaster stood up to announce the exam results.

i that we had to open all the windows.

j in case it gets colder later on.

k as soon as he got to his hotel.

l although he could easily afford it.

m provided that the weather stays fine.

n if you pick me up from work.

o unless I work a lot harder.

p as long as you fill it up with petrol.

1	2	3	4	5	6	7	8	9	10	11	12	13	14	15	16

(b) Now complete the sentences below with a suitable conjunction. Choose from the ones found in (a).

1 Of course you can borrow my CDs, ... you bring them back.

2 Everyone in the theatre rose .... the Queen entered the royal box.

3 Take an umbrella with you .... it rains.

4 .... being deaf, Beethoven went on composing music.

5 I was given the blame .... it wasn't my fault.

6 You'll feel perfectly at home in France .... you've picked up the language.

7 He won't play for our club .... we pay him.

8 We didn't go on holiday this year .... we couldn't afford it.

9 .... you don't try, then how do you know you can't do it?

10 I wouldn't go out with her .... she was the last woman on earth!

41 Sentence-changing 6

Complete the second sentence so that it has a similar meaning to the first one. Use one of the words in the box on the left plus a preposition. (Most of the prepositions will be used more than once.) There is an example at the beginning (0).

air	order	by
average	purpose	in
debt	random	at
first sight	short	on
good	stock	for
heart	the moment	out of
myself	the house	
once	work	

0   We flew to Paris.
    We went to Paris .... *by air* ....

1   Come here immediately!
    Come here ....!

2   My name's Patrick, but most people call me Pat.
    My name's Patrick. Pat ....

3   Most people in this country work forty hours a week.
    .... people in this country work forty hours a week.

4   He left Russia in 1992 and will never go back there.
    He left Russia .... in 1992.

5   We'll have to use the stairs. The lift's not working.
    We'll have to use the stairs. The lift's ....

6   Mr Blake comes back from his holiday next week.
    Mr Blake is on holiday ....

7   He owes the bank £5,000.
    He is £5,000 ....

8 I memorized the poem.
   I learnt the poem ....

9 It was no accident. He did it deliberately.
   It was no accident. He did it ....

10 He hasn't had a job for over two years.
   He's been .... for over two years.

11 I fell in love with her the moment I saw her.
   It was love ....

12 No one helped me with the homework.
   I did the homework ....

13 The goods you want won't come in until next week.
   The goods you want are .... at the moment.

14 'You don't have to pay for the drinks – they're free tonight,' said the hotel manager.
   'The drinks are .... tonight,' said the hotel manager.

15 When you play bingo, the numbers are not called out in any particular order.
   When you play bingo, the numbers are called out ....

42 Choose the answer 4

Read the text below and decide which word **a**, **b**, **c** or **d** best fits each space. There is an example at the beginning (0).

Safer driving with hands off

SCIENTISTS are developing cars which **(0)** ... hands-free driving on British motorways.

Computers will be **(1)** ... to sensors to control steering, speed and braking.

Drivers will **(2)** ... push a button to let the car take the strain.

Automatic steering systems will **(3)**... cars in lane.

Cruise control will keep speeds at a steady level by opening or closing the **(4)** ....

Ultrasonic anti-collision devices will **(5)** ... safe, efficient distances between vehicles, **(6)** ... operating brakes.

Research is being **(7)** ... by Professor John Turner, head of Automotive Engineering at Southampton University and by experts **(8)** ... in Britain and overseas.

The work reflects a global increase in traffic **(9)** ... motorways.

Cameras

A Transport Department report last week showed that car **(10)** ... in London **(11)** ... by 20 per cent in the last ten years, putting **(12)** ... strain on motorways.

British experts have already found a way to keep cars in lane **(13)** ... driver control. 'The system uses TV cameras at the front of the car, which **(14)**... up white lane markings,' says Turner. 'Images are **(15)** ... into computers linked to the steering mechanism.'

'The problem now is **(16)** ... the cost and weight of the equipment.'

Expensive cruise-control devices are also being **(17)** ...

If all cars were programmed to travel at say, 65 mph experts believe **(18)** ... more vehicles would be able to use the motorways without traffic jams and in greater safety.

Professor Turner's team at Southampton is also engaged **(19)** ... research with Ford in collision-**(20)** ... systems using radar and ultrasonic equipment.

0 a let	b provide	c allow	d devise
1 a powered	b linked	c fed	d combined
2 a simply	b effectively	c casually	d effortlessly

3 a hold	b sustain	c keep	d retain
4 a brake	b throttle	c clutch	d valves
5 a provide	b be allowed	c insist	d maintain
6 a even	b although	c without	d simply
7 a made	b carried out	c operated	d looked into
8 a overall	b elsewhere	c scientists	d throughout
9 a stopping	b gripping	c clogging	d obstructing
10 a journeys	b routes	c travels	d tours
11 a will increase	b rose	c have mounted	d had risen
12 a spacious	b extensive	c immense	d large
13 a without	b outperforming	c solely	d providing
14 a show	b pick	c beam	d reflect
15 a linked	b sorted	c classified	d fed
16 a lowering	b to sink	c to reduce	d deducting
17 a changed	b purified	c adopted	d refined
18 a lot	b much	c many	d various
19 a at	b with	c for	d in
20 a avoidance	b preventing	c aversion	d evasion

43 Word-building 3

Use the word given in capitals at the end of each line to form a word that fits the space in the same line. There is an example at the beginning (0).

The Elephant Man

John Merrick was one of the most **(0)** ... human	ORDINARY
beings who ever lived. He suffered from a rare bone	
disease which **(1)** ... him grotesquely: his right	FORM
arm was like a giant claw, his right leg was nearly	
twice the normal size. His head was **(2)** ... and	LARGE
misshapen, and his scaly skin reeked of a peculiar	
odour. When young he had a 9-inch **(3)** ... protruding	GROW
from his mouth, which gave rise to the nickname 'The	
Elephant Man'. Although it was removed when he	
was fourteen, the **(4)** ... name stayed with him.	FORTUNE
Merrick made a **(5)** ... living as a freak in a peep	REASON
show. It was there that he was seen by the eminent	
surgeon, Frederick Treeves. Merrick's **(6)** ...	PAIN
deformities disturbed and fascinated Treeves. He took	
him into his private care, set up an apartment for him in	
the London Hospital and gave him a mask to wear	
while walking the halls so as not to **(7)** ... other	FEAR
patients and staff.	
Treeves soon discovered that 'The Elephant Man'	
had considerable **(8)** ... and spoke like a poet.	INTELLIGENT
Treeves's friends began to visit Merrick, initially	
to look, but in time to talk. Merrick never	
complained of his pain and **(9)** ..., but always kept	SUFFER
his and others' spirits high. His reputation spread.	
Members of the Royal Family, **(10)** ... Princess	PARTICULAR
Alexandra, were among those who **(11)** ... visited	REPEAT
him.	
The **(12)** ... of his soul had escaped the prison	BEAUTIFUL
of his body, but his **(13)** ... continued to progress. As	ILL
he became weaker, walking became an exhausting	
process, and he was forced to spend more and more	

time in bed. Because of the huge **(14)** ... of his head,
he could only sleep sitting up. One night, at the age
of twenty seven, Merrick laid his head down and died.
Among the few things he left behind were these lines of
verse, written **(15)** ... before his death:

> Was I so tall I could reach the pole
> or grasp the ocean with a span
> I would be measured by the soul
> the mind's the measure of the man.

Merrick's skeleton, preserved in the London
Hospital, is **(16)** ... of the terrible disease from
which he suffered. It also gives testimony to the
(17) ... of man.

WEIGH

SHORT

PROVE

DIGNIFIED

Write your answers here.

1	*extraordinary*	7		13	
2		8		14	
3		9		15	
4		10		16	
5		11		17	
6		12			

44 One word only 4

Read the text below and think of the word which best fits each space. Use only **one** word in each space. There is an example at the beginning (0).

Call Me Mother

It was **(0)**... first wedding anniversary and to celebrate it Colin and his wife, Julie, decided to go **(1)**... a meal at one of the **(2)**... expensive restaurants in town. They were **(3)**... the romantic evening, gazing lovingly **(4)**... each other's eyes, when an elderly lady sitting alone made her way to their table.

I'm terribly sorry to **(5)**... you,' she said, wiping away a tear. 'But you look just **(6)**... my son. He was killed in a car accident just over a year ago and I **(7)**... miss him terribly. I wonder if you'd **(8)**... me a favour?'

The couple were very moved by the old lady and, feeling sorry **(9)**... her, agreed to help if they could.

'I wonder if, just as I'm leaving, you **(10)**... say "Goodbye, Mum" and wave me off? It would give me **(11)**... a thrill.'

'Of course we will,' the couple replied. 'No problem.' Well, **(12)**... could they possibly refuse?

The old lady thanked them and went back to her table. **(13)**... a short while, she picked up all her belongings and got up to leave.

'Goodbye, Mum!' shouted the couple with a big, theatrical wave as the old lady made her way slowly out **(14)**... the restaurant. 'See you at the weekend,' Colin added.

Feeling very pleased **(15)**... they had made an old person happy, they finished their meal and asked for the **(16)**.... But after checking and rechecking it they sent for the manager, demanding to know **(17)**... they had been overcharged by more than £40.

'But that **(18)**... the charge for the lady's meal,' the manager explained. 'She said her son would pay.'

Write your answers here.

0 .....*their*.....	5	10	15 ....
1	6	11	16 ....
2	7	12	17 ....
3	8	13	18 ....
4	9	14	

45 Fill in the missing prepositions (*various*)

Fill in the missing prepositions (or adverb particles) in the following passage. There is an example at the beginning (0).

The Curse of Tutankhamun

Most people scoff **(0)**... the idea of curses coming true, but the events that followed the opening **(1)**... Tutankhamun's tomb **(2)**... Howard Carter **(3)**... 1922 may make them think twice **(4)**... laughing.

The story **(5)**... the curse began when the last man climbed out **(6)**... the tomb. It is said that a sudden sandstorm blew **(7)**... and that the men **(8)**... the party saw a hawk, the ancient royal symbol **(9)**... Egypt, fly overhead.

Local Egyptians took this to mean that the spirit **(10)**... the dead king had left his tomb, cursing those who had opened it. Five months later, the man who financed the expedition, Lord Carnarvon, was bitten **(11)**... the cheek **(12)**... a mosquito. Normally nothing too serious! But the bite became infected and Carnarvon caught pneumonia and died **(13)**... an Egyptian hospital.

(14)... the precise moment **(15)**... his death all the lights **(16)**... Cairo went **(17)**..., and thousands **(18)**... miles away **(19)**... the Carnarvon mansion **(20)**... Hampshire, England, his dog began to howl – and died **(21)**... the night. Doctors who examined the mummified body **(22)**... Tutankhamun reported that he had a small depression **(23)**... his cheek, just like a mosquito bite, **(24)**... exactly the same spot where Carnarvon had been bitten.

Many people who visited the tomb also died **(25)**... strange circumstances. Lord Carnarvon's half-brother died **(26)**... a burst appendix. An Egyptian prince whose family claimed descent **(27)**... the pharaohs was murdered **(28)**... London and his brother committed suicide. An American railway tycoon caught a cold while **(29)**... the tomb and died **(30)**... pneumonia.

The man who helped Howard Carter to catalogue the items found **(31)**... the tomb committed suicide, and a few months later his father jumped **(32)**... his death **(33)**... the balcony **(34)**... his London flat. There was an alabaster vase **(35)**... the tomb **(36)**... the room that he jumped **(37)**....

(38)... 1966 the government **(39)**... Egypt agreed to lend the treasures **(40)**... France **(41)**... an important exhibition. The Director **(42)**... Antiquities fought **(43)**...

the decision, because he had dreamed that he would die if he allowed the treasures to go **(44)**... (*two words*) Egypt. When he left the last meeting, still trying to make the authorities change their minds, he was knocked down **(45)**... a car and died two days later.

And Howard Carter who was the first man **(46)**... the tomb? He died – **(47)**... natural causes – **(48)**... 1939.

Write your answers here.

0 ...... *at*	13	26	39 ....
1	14	27	40 ....
2	15	28	41 ....
3	16	29	42 ....
4	17	30	43 ....
5	18	31	44 ....
6	19	32	45 ....
7	20	33	46 ....
8	21	34	47 ....
9	22	35	48 ....
10	23	36	
11	24	37	
12	25	38	

46 Position of adjectives and adverbs

(a) Put the adjectives in the correct places and in the right order in the following sentences. There is an example at the beginning (0).

0 She bought a handbag in the sale. (*leather, brown*)

　　She bought a brown leather handbag in the sale.

1 He bought a bunch of roses. (*yellow, sweet-smelling*)

　　...

2 She was very attractive with long hair. (*blonde, lovely*)

　　...

3 The hotel was owned by a businessman. (*fat, German, middle-aged*)

　　...

4 They lived in a house. (*modern, brick, three-bedroomed, detached*)

　　...

5 My brother loves sports cars. (*red, Italian, fast*)

　　...

6 In the middle of the room was a coffee table. (*oval, superb, oak*)

　　...

7 Where did you get this vase from? (*old, magnificent, Japanese*)

　　...

8 I love meals. (*tasty, hot, Indian*)

　　...

9 He was wearing a jacket. (*shabby, brown, old, corduroy*)

　　...

10 Outside the Town Hall was a statue. (*marble, huge, triangular, black*)

　　...

(b) Put the adverbs in the best places in the following sentences. There is an example at the beginning (0).

0 He gets up early at weekends. (*usually*)

   <u>He usually gets up early at weekends</u>

1 I play tennis on Saturdays. (*sometimes*)

   ....

2 Do you go out at weekends? (*usually*)

   ....

3 Carol's daughter plays the violin. (*beautifully*)

   ....

4 My brother finishes work on Fridays. (*always, early*)

   ....

5 I don't go to the theatre. My sister, on the other hand, goes. (*often, regularly*)

   ....

6 I don't understand why Joanna didn't want to come to my party. (*still*)

   ....

7 I haven't done much work so I'll fail the exam. (*probably*)

   ....

8 I disagree with you! Irish people are friendlier than English people. (*completely, definitely*)

   ....

9 'Where's Rose?'
   'She's gone home.' (*just*)

   ....

10 David's got three children and they are musical. (*all*)

   ....

47 Phrasal verbs (*various*)

Read through the pairs of sentences below, then decide which phrasal verb can be used to replace the words in italics in both. There is an example at the beginning (0).

0 (a) I can't decide which dress to *wear*.
  (b) I *gained* almost a kilo in weight when I was on holiday.
  Phrasal verb: ..*put on*..

1 (a) I *learnt to speak* French when I worked in France one summer.
  (b) The Prime Minister announced that there were signs that the economy was really *showing signs of recovery*.
  Phrasal verb: ....

2 (a) Are you sure I'm not *inconveniencing you*?
  (b) It took the firemen three hours to *extinguish* the fire.
  Phrasal verb: ....

3 (a) He spoke with such a broad Scottish accent that the students found it really difficult to *understand* what he was saying.
  (b) I asked him to *write out* the cheque to Celtic Enterprises.
  Phrasal verb: ....

4 (a) When he deliberately punched the other team's goalkeeper, the referee *ordered him to leave the field*.
  (b) Have you *written to them requesting* their latest catalogue yet?
  Phrasal verb: ....

5 (a) The cost of the new bridge could *reach a figure of* millions of pounds.
  (b) The car *collided with* a lorry just outside the station.
  Phrasal verb: ....

6 (a) You should always *make a copy of* important files on your computer, preferably every day.
  (b) If I tell the boss we're not prepared to work overtime this weekend will the rest of you *support me*?
  Phrasal verb: ....

7 (a) I don't think the new fashion will really *become popular*.
  (b) She's very gullible and didn't *realize what was happening* for quite a while.
  Phrasal verb: ....

8 (a) He *didn't accept* the job because the salary was too low.

  (b) The radio's very loud. *Reduce the sound*, please.

    Phrasal verb: ....

9 (a) I shall *decorate and repair* this old house and then sell it.

  (b) My hands were so cold that I couldn't *fasten* my top button.

    Phrasal verb: ....

10 (a) The old man *donated* half his fortune to charity.

  (b) They'll never believe you're French. Your accent will *betray you*.

    Phrasal verb: ....

11 (a) They *started their journey* early in the morning to avoid the traffic.

  (b) The cakes were *arranged* on a trolley, and looked really delicious.

    Phrasal verb: ....

12 (a) Could you help me to *inflate* these balloons?

  (b) The terrorists *destroyed* the building *with dynamite*.

    Phrasal verb: ....

13 (a) My father was *summoned to join the army* soon after the war began.

  (b) How many times have I told you never to *telephone me* at work!

    Phrasal verb: ....

14 (a) I'm too fat! I'd better *stop eating* biscuits and chocolates.

  (b) You should always *surrender* your seat on a bus to an old or disabled person.

    Phrasal verb: ....

15 (a) Two masked men *stopped and robbed* a security van and stole over £300,000.

  (b) The train was *delayed* for two hours because of an accident on the line.

    Phrasal verb: ....

48 Make, do or have

(a) Place the following words under the correct headings.

a bank account	a driving lesson	one's best
a barbecue	fun of someone	a phone call
a bath/shower	a fuss	a profit/loss
the bed	the garden	research
business	harm	the shopping
a celebration	an impression	someone a favour
a complaint	a journey	a speech
a confession	a mistake	
damage	a noise	

Make	Do	Have
1	1	1 ....
2	2	2 ....
3	3	3 ....
4	4	4 ....
5	5	5 ....
6	6	
7	7	
8	8	
9		
10		
11		
12		

(b) Now fill in the gaps in the following sentences with the correct form of *make, do* or *have*.

1 Why do politicians always take so long to .... decisions?

2 It's time you .... a holiday, Margaret. It will .... you the world of good.

3 Everyone over the age of thirty should .... a will.

4 Your daughter is .... excellent progress, Mrs Grove. She ought to .... well in next year's exams.

5 It .... no difference to me when you finish it, as long as you .... a good job.

6 I've decided to .... a big party on my birthday. Could I leave you to .... the arrangements, darling?

7 You must .... the exam, I'm afraid. You .... no alternative.

8 The two countries .... talks last week and are optimistic about .... peace soon.

9 Take this medicine. It will .... you good.

10 This photograph doesn't .... Sally justice. She's much better-looking really.

11 If we are going to .... this company profitable again we are going to have to .... a lot of changes.

12 She .... an appointment to .... her eyes tested.

13 Do you mind if I .... a suggestion?

14 I .... a really good time at the party and .... lots of friends.

15 I hope you don't think I'm .... excuses, but I really must stay in tonight and .... my hair.

16 'How's Sylvia getting on in America?'
   'Oh, she's .... the time of her life. In fact, she's .... plans to settle there.'

17 'You see your parents quite often. You must .... a good relationship with them.'
   'No, not really. It's more a question of .... one's duty.'

18 We moved closer together to .... room for Annie to sit down.

19 Volvo .... a very good reputation for quality and safety.

20 They .... us a very good offer for our flat.

49 Sentence-changing 7

Complete the second sentence so that it has a similar meaning to the first sentence, using phrasal verbs and other words in your answer. **Do not change the word given.** You must use between two and five words, including the word given. There is an example at the beginning (0).

0 Terrorists tried to destroy the bridge using dynamite.
   blow
   Terrorists tried ....*to blow up*.......... the bridge.

1 He went to Spain to try to speak Spanish better.
   brush
   He went to Spain .... Spanish.

2 Is she Australian?
   come
   .... Australia?

3 Ask Paul to do it. You can rely on him.
   let
   Ask Paul to do it. He ....

4 It's a very formal dinner party.
   dress
   We are expected .... for the dinner party.

5 An ankle injury prevented her from taking part in the race.
   drop
   She had to .... the race because of an ankle injury.

6 It was nearly midnight when John arrived.
   turn
   John .... until nearly midnight.

7 I'm not very confident of passing my driving test.
   get
   I don't .... my driving test.

8 The meeting went on until 11.30.
   break
   The meeting .... until 11.30.

9 Unless business improves soon, we'll be bankrupt by the end of the year.
   pick
   If business .... soon, we'll be bankrupt by the end of the year.

10 The last time my rent rose was three years ago.
   put
   They haven't .... for three years.

11 You will support me at the meeting, won't you?
   back
   You will .... at the meeting, won't you?

12 This form must be completed before you leave.
   fill
   You .... this form before you leave.

13 I don't think I'll go out on Saturday.
   stay
   I think .... on Saturday.

14 Unless it stops raining soon, we'll have to cancel the picnic.
   clear
   If it .... soon we'll have to cancel the picnic.

15 I don't smoke as many cigarettes as I used to.
   cut
   I've managed to .... cigarettes I smoke.

50 What's wrong? 2

Only four of the sentences below are grammatically correct. Find these four sentences and rewrite those that contain mistakes.

1 Not only he writes books but he also paints.

....

2 Excuse me for not write sooner, but I've been very busy lately.

....

3 I thought you said you were going to give up smoking?

....

4 Always she is arriving late for work.

....

5 Everyone were late because of the bad weather.

....

6 You mustn't do it. It's voluntary.

....

7 I was just sixteen years when I first fell in love.

....

8 If I had asked you to marry me would you have said yes?

....

9 You look beautifully, Jane. That dress really suits you.

....

10 I like very much pop music, but my brother doesn't.

....

11 Turn that music down, will you? I've got the headache.

....

12 It's late! It's time we all went home.

....

13 I'll just say goodnight to Robert then I'll bring you home.

....

14 Did you enjoy at the party last night?

....

15 Could you explain me how to use a computer?

....

16 I have few interest in sport. My main hobby is train-spotting.

....

17 We've been married since seven years now.

....

18 Do you like something to eat now?

....

19 Mr Brown doesn't work any more here, I'm afraid.

....

20 Doesn't she have something to do with the BBC?

....

Answers

1 Sentence-changing 1
(*Suggestion*)
1 did not/didn't expect to
2 is famous for (its)
3 take no notice of
4 died at the age of/only reach-
   ed the age of
5 put you up
6 left without saying
7 apologized for being
8 might not/mightn't have got
9 ago I gave up
10 should not/shouldn't have
   stolen
11 takes four hours to travel
12 'd rather not/would rather
   not

2 The definite and indefinite article
1 The, an, the, – 2 a, the, a
3 The, the, the, – 4 –, –, the 5 a,
the, an, –, the 6 –, a, –, the 7 a,
–, the, the 8 –, the – 9 –, the,
The, the, –, the 10 an, –, a, the

3 One word only 1
(*Suggestion*)
1 much/far ... with ... than
2 been ... since
3 When ... used ... on
4 often/frequently ... a/every
5 as/so ... better/cleverer
6 can't/couldn't/didn't
   ... because/ as
7 started ... ago ... still
8 for ... like
9 yours ... not ... don't/can't
10 going/hoping/planning ...
   leave
11 long ... get/drive/travel ... by
12 It ... there
13 since ... yet
14 did ... last/do ... at
15 much/usually ... than
16 All/Most/Half ... only/not
17 many ... were
18 What ... almost/nearly/exactly/
   approximately/about
19 do ... really ... did ... all
20 have ... if ... in

21 been ... is/will be
22 ago ... there
23 would ... had ... more
24 can't ... for

4 Identifying Grammatical terms and verb tenses
(*a*)
adjective 6
adverb of manner 16
adverb of frequency 8
auxiliary verb 20
comparative 1
conjunction 13
definite article 12
gerund 15
idiom 18
indefinite article 2
interrogative pronoun 9
modal verb 5
personal pronoun 17
phrasal verb 11
possessive pronoun 14
preposition 7
present participle 3
question tag 19
reflexive pronoun 10
time expression 4

(*b*)
conditional 3
future 8
future continuous 10
future perfect 6
imperative 14
passive 1
past continuous 4
past perfect 9
past perfect continuous 12
present continuous 15
present continuous with future
meaning 5
present perfect 11
present perfect continuous 2
present simple 13
present simple with future
meaning 7

5 Fill in the verbs
1 had been stolen 2 phoned
3 leaving 4 returned 5 found

6 had been brought back 7 was
8 opened 9 found 10 apologiz-
ing 11 had written 12 did not
have/didn't have 13 had gone
14 hoped 15 did not mind/did-
n't mind/ wouldn't mind 16 had
taken 17 enclosed 18 were
19 had been trying/had tried
20 had 21 had expected 22 were
23 decided 24 got 25 awaited
26 had been burgled 27 had
been stolen 28 knew 29 lying
30 recognized 31 saying
32 enjoyed

6 Choose the answer 1: Verbs and adjectives
1 b 2 a 3 c 4 b 5 d 6 b 7 c 8 c
9 a 10 d 11 b 12 b 13 c 14 a
15 b 16 a 17 d 18 c
19 d 20 c

7 Phrasal verbs 1: Break, bring, call
(*a*)
1 broken off 2 broke in 3 broke
out 4 break up 5 broke away

(*b*)
1 brought on 2 bring back/in
3 bring up 4 bring out 5 brings
back

(*c*)
1 call for 2 call ... up 3 call off
4 call on 5 called ... after

(*d*)
1 break out 2 call for 3 bring
up 4 call on 5 break down
6 bring on 7 call up 8 break in
9 call off 10 bring back

8 What's the question?
(*Suggestion*)
1 How often does she see her
   sister?
2 Where does Judy's husband
   work?
3 How much does Paul weigh?/
   What's Paul's weight?/What

does Paul weigh?/How heavy is Paul?

4 What did she buy in the sales?

5 How long has David lived in Brighton?/Since when has David lived in Brighton?

6 Why did they arrest him?/What did they arrest him for?/Why was he arrested?/What was he arrested for?

7 Which language did your mother speak fluently as a child?/What language did your mother speak fluently as a child?/What did your mother speak fluently as a child?

8 What colour hair does Jill have?/What's the colour of Jill's hair?

9 Who did this pen once belong to?/Who did this pen used to belong to?/Who once owned this pen?/Who used to own this pen?

10 What sort of car does Jane have?/What make of car does Jane have?/What kind of car does Jane have?

11 How did he pay for the goods?

12 How many times a week do you play tennis?

13 Where did she meet her boyfriend?

14 What does he always have for breakfast?

15 How long did you have to wait to get through customs?/How long did you wait to get through customs?

16 Whose brother is a famous soccer player?

17 How far is Cardiff from Swansea?/How many miles is Cardiff from Swansea?

18 What time did you finally get home last night?

9 Fill the gaps 1 (*Suggestion*)
1 you see/you should see/you happen to see
2 Is it far/Is it a long way
3 Are you going/Have you been

invited
4 should turn/have to turn
5 Unless you work/If you don't work
6 get used to/get accustomed to/feel confident at
7 will take (us)
8 didn't know/didn't realize/wasn't aware/had no idea that
9 'd better/had better/ought to/(really) must
10 have you had
11 I come from/I was born in/I'm from
12 would you do/buy/say, etc./would you feel like
13 must have cost
14 don't forget to take/remember to take/(perhaps) you'd better take/I suggest you take
15 can't/mustn't/'d better not

10 Find the mistakes 1
1 she 2 of 3 ✓ 4 will 5 it 6 ✓
7 that 8 the 9 ✓ 10 ✓ 11 then 12 try 13 ✓ 14 for 15 not 16 very

11 Word order
1 Do you know if Peter Smith works here?

2 Excuse me, could you tell me the way to the station, please?

3 Is there any chance of having the day off tomorrow?

4 How often do you borrow books from the library?

5 Did you remember to post that letter I gave you?

6 Have you ever been to Spain or any other Mediterranean country?

7 If I promise not to step on your toes, will you dance with me?/Will you dance with me if I promise not to step on your toes?

8 Are either of you interested in playing a round of golf this weekend?

9 Do you sometimes wonder what life is all about?/Do you wonder sometimes what life is all about?

10 Are there any tickets left for Saturday's performance of

Cats?

11 What time does the bus leave and can you smoke on it?

12 Which of you forgot to switch the light off last night before you went to bed?/Which of you forgot to switch the light off before you went to bed last night?/Which of you forgot to switch off the light last night before you went to bed?/Which of you forgot to switch off the light before you went to bed last night?

12 Sentence-changing 2
(*Suggestion*)
1 to take care of/to care for
2 now to get over
3 doesn't live (very) far from/lives not very far from
4 was such a boring programme
5 don't approve of (us)
6 prevented us from driving
7 regrets selling/regrets having sold
8 is supposed to
9 the time everyone left
10 is bored by/with
11 give a/any reason for arriving
12 made it difficult (for her)

13 Question words
1 Where 2 By which/what 3 Why/After whom 4 To which/what 5 What 6 Who 7 On which/what 8 What 9 From which/what 10 How many 11 With which/what 12 Whose 13 In which/what 14 How old 15 Which/What

1 a 2 c 3 c 4 b 5 c 6 a 7 c 8 b 9 c 10 a 11 b 12 c 13 a 14 c 15 b

14 One word only 2
(*Suggestion*)
1 from 2 decided/wanted/hoped/intended 3 later/afterwards 4 about/with 5 into/through 6 his 7 rather 8 took 9 belonging 10 but 11 on 12 after 13 back 14 no/few

15 would 16 of 17 saw/met/spotted 18 how 19 some/a 20 has

15 Prepositions after adjectives

1 fond of (keen on) 2 ill with 3 responsible for 4 serious about 5 terrified of 6 absent from 7 eligible for 8 friendly with 9 proud of 10 rich in 11 short of 12 absorbed in 13 famous for 14 good at 15 keen on (fond of) 16 satisfied with 17 similar ... to 18 grateful to 19 jealous of 20 cruel to

16 What's wrong? 1

1 We are much better than them at football./We are much better than they are at football.
2 Correct
3 My parents have lived in Ireland since 1985./My parents have been living in Ireland since 1985.
4 He had such a broad Scottish accent that I had difficulty in understanding him at first.
5 The prize money was shared among the four of them. (Between *is used with two people.*)
6 You'd feel a lot better if you gave up smoking.
7 Can you tell me where the post office is, please?
8 In my opinion, neither of the candidates is really suitable.
9 Bananas are my favourite fruit.
10 Correct
11 I've had a tiring day. I think I'll go to bed early tonight.
12 They told me that they would arrive on Friday evening.
13 Both girls had blonde hair and blue eyes./Both of the girls had blonde hair and blue eyes.
14 We look forward to hearing from you soon.
15 No sooner had the tennis match started than it began to rain.
16 Correct
17 Of the three sisters, she was the best singer. (Better *is used when you compare two people.*)
18 Did you have a lot of rain last week?
19 Correct
20 David should have arrived at 2 o'clock, but he didn't turn up.

17 Phrasal verbs 2: Come, cut, fall

(a)
1 came across 2 come round/to 3 came in 4 come into 5 come out

(b)
1 cut down 2 cut ... out 3 cut up 4 cut back 5 cut off

(c)
1 fell down 2 fallen out 3 fell in 4 fell through 5 fall for

(d)
1 come into 2 cut up 3 fall through 4 come out 5 fall for 6 come across 7 cut down 8 cut off 9 come round/to 10 fall out

18 Choose the answer 2: Various words

1 b 2 c (*in the suburbs*) 3 b 4 d 5 a 6 d 7 b 8 c (*make a fuss*) 9 a 10 b 11 a 12 d 13 c 14 a 15 c 16 d 17 c 18 b 19 d 20 c

19 Sentence-changing 3
(*Suggestion*)
1 did not/didn't start eating until
2 wish I could/wish I knew how to
3 in order not to meet/in order to avoid (meeting)
4 are different from
5 last heard from Sally
6 insisted on us staying/that we stayed
7 turns out
8 had not/hadn't behaved badly
9 does not/doesn't matter to me

to rain.

10 would prefer/'d prefer not to
11 if he felt like playing
12 and immediately switched on

20 What's missing? 1
(*Suggestion*)
The words in brackets show where in the line the missing word should appear.

1 ✓ 2 would (/appear in) 3 my (of/most) 4 ✓ 5 had (I/gone) 6 a (as/receptionist) 7 ✓ 8 in (/difficulty/finding) 9 park (car/and) 10 when (space/a) 11 ✓ 12 angry, annoyed, furious, mad, irate, etc. (really/so) 13 at (swore/him) 14 which (away,/of) 15 because (difficulties,/it) 16 ✓ 17 could (I/find) 18 By (space./This) 19 ✓ 20 at, on (knocked/the) 21 and, who (man/was) 22 almost, nearly (I/died) 23 in (at/the) 24 ✓ 25 the (saw/funny) 26 getting (/the job) 27 not (/to shout)

21 Word-building 1
1 admission 2 analysis 3 appointment 4 beauty 5 arguments 6 confidence 7 inconvenience 8 decision 9 disappointment 10 inquiries 11 explanation 12 frequency 13 unhappiness 14 imagination 15 knowledge 16 musician 17 possibility 18 stupidity 19 violence 20 warmth

22 Infinitive or -ing form?
1 to hurt 2 to play 3 thinking 4 to leave 5 saving 6 wanting 7 to like 8 giving 9 meeting 10 to stay 11 talking 12 getting 13 to teach 14 to win 15 taking 16 being 17 to walk 18 to pass 19 to see 20 living

23 Some or any combinations
(*Suggestion*)
1 anyone/anybody 2 some any 3 Someone/Somebody anywhere 4 Anything some any 5 some something 6 any something any 7 some Someone/Somebody any 8 somewhere Anywhere something 9 anywhere (*possibly* some-

where) some 10 some any 11 any some 12 any some

24 One word only 3 ✓
(*Suggestion*)

1 as/while 2 trying/hoping/waiting 3 So 4 come 5 without 6 would 7 pulled/drove/drew 8 room 9 surprise/horror/amazement/disgust/annoyance/delight, etc. (*any suitable abstract noun*) 10 As/ Since/Because 11 inside 12 made 13 long 14 had 15 pick 16 out 17 get/feel 18 of/off 19 been 20 with 21 off/from 22 since/again ✓

25 Prepositions after verbs

1 insure ... against 2 remind ... of 3 think ... about 4 apologize for 5 charged with 6 protect ... from 7 succeeded in 8 written by 9 believe in 10 share ... among 11 complimented ... on 12 lost at 13 arrived in 14 smelled of 15 suffers from 16 feel sorry for 17 care for 18 prefer ... to 19 rely on 20 translated into

26 Sentence-changing 4
(*Suggestion*)

1 Would you care for
2 this pen belong to
3 wasn't/was not well/fit enough
4 must be over eighteen
5 's/is time we went/were going
6 's/is the last time
7 wish I'd/I had got
8 had difficulty in starting
9 did she refuse to
10 haven't/have not fallen out
11 can't/cannot have seen
12 there was still no sign

27 Phrasal verbs 3: Get, go, keep
(*a*)
1 get back 2 got in 3 get at 4 get through 5 getting ... down

(*b*)
1 went through 2 go by 3 gone off 4 go with 5 went out

(*c*)

1 keep off 2 keep up with 3 keep away 4 keep on 5 keeping ... back

(*d*)

1 get through 2 go with 3 keep up with 4 get on/along 5 go out 6 get back 7 keep back 8 go off 9 get down 10 go by

28 Find the mistakes 2
1 following 2 ✓ 3 so 4 ✓ 5 when 6 that 7 come 8 an 9 ✓ 10 as 11 after 12 ✓ 13 inside 14 out 15 ✓ 16 have 17 for

29 Fill the gaps 2
(*Suggestion*)

1 should have been/were supposed to be/ought to have been
2 wouldn't have been able to/would not have been able to
3 stopped smoking/gave up smoking/gave them up
4 have to go/have to leave
5 not used to/not accustomed to/incapable of
6 one of the nicest/kindest/most pleasant/most interesting, most intelligent, etc.
7 or you'll/or you will/or you might/in case you
8 've had/have had/'ve drunk/have drunk
9 wouldn't have got/would not have got/wouldn't have arrived/would not have arrived
10 not to have/to cancel/they wouldn't have/they would not have/to postpone/to call off/to put off
11 does she (Mary, your sister, etc.) do for
12 will have been working
13 haven't seen/have not seen/haven't spoken to/have not spoken to/haven't heard a word from/have not heard a word from
14 I'd gone/I had gone/I'd chosen/I had chosen/I'd spent it/I had spent it/we'd gone/we had gone/we'd cho-

sen/we had chosen/we'd spent it/we had spent it
15 can't (possibly)/cannot (possibly)/couldn't (possibly)/ could not (possibly)
16 before she was able to/before she could
17 can't come/cannot come/aren't able to come/are not able to come/don't want to come/do not want to come/aren't interested in coming/are not interested in coming/won't be coming/will not be coming
18 as soon as/once/the minute/after/when
19 It's been/It has been
20 'd rather/would rather/'d prefer to/would prefer to
21 wouldn't have/would not have/might not have
22 me a ring/bell/call
23 Unless you/If you don't
24 she took/she had taken
25 do you borrow/do you take out/do you read

30 What's missing? 2
(*Suggestion*)

1 own (had her/) 2 the (in/sights) 3 ✓ 4 ✓ 5 down, along (strolled/ the) 6 and (/saw the) 7 When (/she returned) 8 ✓ 9 having (ever/been) 10 ✓ 11 her (/mother check) 12 ✓ 13 later (years/in) 14 never (hospital,/having) 15 After (explanation?/the daughter) 16 ✓ 17 that (doctor/ she) 18 not (instructed/to) 19 fled, left (visitors/the) 20 ✓ 21 another, a (and/couple) 22 to (happened/the)

31 Broken sentences 1
(*if-clauses*)
(*a*)
1 p 2 k 3 g 4 n 5 j 6 d 7 a 8 m 9 f 10 o 11 i 12 l 13 h 14 b 15 e 16 c
(*b*)
1 rains 2 would lose 3 would not/wouldn't have taken 4 will you pay 5 would not/wouldn't have happened 6 will not/won't

come 7 practised 8 will lose 9 had not/hadn't/braked 10 had worked

32 Choose the answer 3
1 c 2 d 3 a 4 c 5 b 6 b 7 c 8 a 9 d 10 c 11 d 12 a 13 d 14 c 15 b 16 c 17 d 18 b

33 Choose the caption
1 c 2 f 3 j 4 h 5 d 6 a 7 i 8 g 9 b 10 e

34 Missing words in a text
1 e 2 j 3 o 4 l 5 h 6 n 7 a 8 c 9 g 10 k 11 b 12 f

35 Prepositional phrases
(a)

AT	first, last, night, once, the moment, work
BY	air, all means, heart, mistake, night, sight
FOR	a change, ever, hire, instance, sale, the moment
IN	a hurry, hospital, order, particular, private, sight, trouble, work
ON	a diet, business, fire, holiday, purpose, sight
OUT OF	breath, date, hospital, order, sight, the ordinary, trouble, work

(b)
1 by all means 2 on business 3 on a diet 4 by sight 5 in hospital 6 out of breath 7 for sale 8 in a hurry 9 for a change 10 at the moment 11 in private 12 by heart 13 on purpose 14 out of order 15 for ever 16 at first

36 Sentence-changing 5
(Suggestion)
1 will get/are getting married
2 you got/had enough sauce
3 are her chances of winning
4 regretted not having gone/ that he hadn't
5 found it difficult to start
6 in case it gets
7 did you pay for

8 every question/all the questions/everything right except
9 doubt if/whether I'll go
10 were grateful to them
11 my uncle's first trip
12 never eaten/tasted better food than

37 Word-building 2
1 ambitious 2 angry 3 artistic 4 careless 5 competitive 6 emotional 7 energetic 8 enjoyable 9 faulty 10 unfriendly 11 frightening 12 harmful 13 homeless 14 icy 15 nervous 16 noisy 17 unreasonable 18 unreliable 19 dissatisfied 20 sensitive 21 ashamed 22 suspicious 23 tasteless 24 useful 25 wooden

38 Phrasal verbs 4: Look, put, take
(a)
1 Look out 2 look forward to 3 look back on 4 look ... up 5 look into

(b)
1 put out 2 put in 3 put by/away/aside 4 put off 5 put down

(c)
1 takes after 2 taking on 3 took to 4 taken in 5 take over

(d)
1 look into 2 take to 3 put by/away/aside 4 look up 5 put out 6 take over 7 put down 8 look after 9 take after 10 look back on

39 More than one meaning
'Extra' meaning (Suggestion)
1 It is bad manners to roll (= *roll about*) in your soup.
2 The adult rather than the bath has a strong bottom.
3 Both the other motorist and a policeman smelled of drink.
4 The farmer was injured with the gun the bull had.
5 The dog is very fond of eating children.

6 They would prefer actors and actresses who had taken drugs.
7 Apart from milking two cows, the woman is also expected to wash and iron them.
8 The woman had a bowl of daffodils between her eyes.
9 The man has to wash two waitresses as well as the dishes.
10 The Queen, not the ship, slid gently into the water.
11 The man, not the saw, has newly sharpened teeth.
12 Boil the baby.

Can be rewritten: (Suggestion only.)
1 It is bad manners to break your bread or break your roll in your soup.
3 Both the motorist involved in the accident and a policeman declared that the other driver smelled of drink.
4 FARMER WITH A GUN WAS INJURED BY AN ANGRY BULL
6 West End Theatre is looking for actors and actresses to perform in a play dealing with the effects of drugs. Previous acting experience preferred.
7 WANTED: a reliable young woman to wash and iron. She will also be required to milk two cows.
9 Busy seaside restaurant requires man to wash dishes. Two waitresses also required.
10 As the ship slid gently into the water, the Queen named her.
12 If your baby does not thrive on raw milk, then boil the milk.

40 Broken sentences 2
(a)
1 i 2 k 3 a 4 g 5 p 6 l 7 m 8 j 9 c 10 h 11 f 12 b 13 d 14 o 15 e 16 n

(b)

1 as long as/provided that 2 as/as soon as 3 in case 4 In spite of 5 even though/although 6 once/as soon as 7 unless/even if 8 because 9 If 10 even if

41 Sentence-changing 6
(*Suggestion*)
1 at once 2 for short 3 On average 4 for good 5 out of order 6 at the moment 7 in debt 8 by heart 9 on purpose 10 out of work 11 at first sight 12 by myself 13 out of stock 14 on the house 15 at random

42 Choose the answer 4
1 b 2 a 3 c 4 b 5 d 6 a 7 b 8 b 9 c 10 a 11 d 12 c 13 a 14 b 15 d 16 c 17 d 18 c 19 d 20 a

43 Word-building 3
1 deformed 2 enlarged 3 growth 4 unfortunate 5 reasonable 6 painful 7 frighten 8 intelligence 9 suffering 10 particularly 11 repeatedly 12 beauty 13 illness 14 weight 15 shortly 16 proof 17 dignity

44 One word only 4
(*Suggestion*)
1 for 2 most/really 3 enjoying/savouring 4 into 5 bother/disturb/trouble 6 like 7 still/do 8 do 9 for 10 would/could/might 11 such 12 how 13 After 14 of 15 that 16 bill 17 why/how 18 includes (*possibly* is *if referring to the £40 extra rather than the whole bill*)

45 Fill in the missing prepositions (*various*)
1 of 2 by 3 in 4 before 5 of 6 of 7 up 8 in 9 of 10 of 11 on 12 by 13 in 14 At 15 of 16 in 17 out 18 of 19 at/in 20 in 21 during/in 22 of 23 on 24 in 25 in/under 26 of 27 from 28 in 29 at/in 30 of 31 in/inside 32 to 33 from 34 of 35 from 36 in 37 from 38 In 39 of 40 to 41 for 42 of 43 against (*no preposition is also possible here*) 44 out of 45 by 46 into/out of

47 of 48 in

46 Position of adjectives and adverbs
(*a*) *Suggestion*
1 He bought a sweet-smelling bunch of yellow roses.
2 She was very attractive with lovely, long, blonde hair.
3 The hotel was owned by a fat, middle-aged, German businessman.
4 They lived in a modern, detached, three-bedroomed, brick house.
5 My brother loves fast, red, Italian sports cars.
6 In the middle of the room was a superb, oval, oak coffee table.
7 Where did you get this magnificent, old Japanese vase from?
8 I love hot, tasty, Indian meals.
9 He was wearing a shabby, old, brown corduroy jacket.
10 Outside the Town Hall was a huge, triangular, black marble statue.

(*b*)
1 I sometimes play tennis on Saturdays./Sometimes I play tennis on Saturdays./I play tennis on Saturdays sometimes.
2 Do you usually go out at weekends?
3 Carol's daughter plays the violin beautifully.
4 My brother always finishes work early on Fridays.
5 I don't often go to the theatre. My sister, on the other hand, goes regularly./I don't go to the theatre often. My sister, on the other hand, goes regularly.
6 I still don't understand why Joanna didn't want to come to my party.
7 I haven't done much work so I'll probably fail the exam.
8 I disagree with you completely!/I completely disagree

with you! Irish people are definitely friendlier than English people.
9 'Where's Rose?'
'She's just gone home.'
10 David's got three children and they are all musical.

47 Phrasal verbs 5 (*various*)
1 pick up (picked up … picking up)
2 put out (putting you out … put out)
3 make out (make out … make out)
4 send off (sent him off … sent off for)
5 run into (run into … ran into)
6 back up (back up … back me up)
7 catch on (catch on … catch on)
8 turn down (turned down … Turn it down)
9 do up (do up … do up)
10 give away (gave away … give you away)
11 set out (set out … set out)
12 blow up (blow up … blew up the building)
13 call up (called up … call me up)
14 give up (give up … give up)
15 hold up (held up … held up)

48 Make, do or have
(*a*)
Make the bed, a complaint, a confession, fun of someone, a fuss, an impression, a journey, a mistake, a noise, a phone call, a profit/loss, a speech

Do business, damage, the garden, harm, one's best, research, the shopping, someone a favour

Have a bank account, a barbecue, a bath/shower, a celebration, a driving lesson
(*b*)

1 make 2 had do 3 make 4 making do 5 makes do 6 have make 7 do have 8 had making 9 do 10 do 11 make make 12 made have 13 make 14 had made 15 making do 16 having making 17 have doing 18 make 19 has/have 20 made

49 Sentence-changing 7
(*Suggestion*)
1 to brush up his
2 Does he come from
3 won't/will not let you down
4 to dress up
5 drop out of
6 didn't/did not turn up
7 think I'll/I will/I shall get through/expect to get through
8 didn't/did not break up
9 doesn't/does not pick up
10 put my rent up/put up my rent
11 back me up
12 must/are required to/are expected to/have to fill in
13 I'll/I will/I shall stay in
14 doesn't/does not clear up
15 cut down the number of

50 What's wrong? 2
1 Not only does he write books but he also paints.
2 Excuse me for not writing sooner, but I've been very busy lately.
3 Correct
4 She is always arriving late for work.
5 Everyone was late because of the bad weather.
6 You needn't do it. It's voluntary./You don't need to do it. It's voluntary./You don't have to do it. It's voluntary.
7 I was just sixteen when I first fell in love./I was just sixteen years old when I first fell in love.
8 Correct.
9 You look beautiful, Jane. That dress really suits you.
10 I like pop music very much, but my brother doesn't.
11 Turn that music down, will you? I've got a headache.
12 Correct.
13 I'll just say goodnight to Robert then I'll take you home.
14 Did you enjoy yourself at the party last night?/Did you enjoy the party last night?
15 Could you explain to me how to use a computer?/Could you explain how to use a computer?
16 I have little interest in sport. My main hobby is train-spotting.
17 We've been married for seven years now.
18 Would you like something to eat now?/Do you want something to eat now?
19 Mr Brown doesn't work here any more, I'm afraid.
20 Correct